BETTER THAN IRL

better than IRL

TRUE STORIES ABOUT FINDING YOUR PEOPLE ON THE UNTAMED INTERNET

*edited by Katie West
and Jasmine Elliott*

&

fiction & feeling

The Pyjarmy © 2020 Erica Buist
I'm From the Internet, Where are You From? © 2020 Mimi Mondal
3 a.m. © 2020 Damien Patrick Williams
In the Flesh © 2020 Sisonke Msimang
Sommy © 2020 Ryan North
To Escape, You Must've Been Brave © 2020 Anaïs Escobar Mathers
Our Second Life © 2020 James Mitchell
Living Between Worlds © 2020 Mohale Mashigo
Under the LJ-Cut: A Love Story © 2020 Kaite Welsh and Lola Keeley
This is Nice. Now Do More © 2020 Leah Reich
The Magic Hotel © 2020 Kyle Cassidy
Monsieur the Middle Man © 2020Randell Zuleka Dauda
I Couldn't Have Been The Only One © 2020 Jon Sung
A Love Letter to the Beautiful Naked Internet Girl of 2013 © 2020 Molly Crabapple
Release The Stars © 2020 Melissa Gira Grant
Staying Vigil © 2020 Catherine Tan
Hold Me Like a Girl © 2020 Jadzia Axelrod
I Was Valkyrie © 2020 Jessica Val Ang
The Beast in Me © 2020 Thomas Pluck
Kayfabe © 2020 Kaitlin Tremblay
The DigiDestined © 2020 Charles Pulliam-Moore
'niichan © 2020 Mel G. Cabrera
The Restaurant at the End of The Internet © 2020 Andy Connor

A CIP record for this book is available from the British Library.

ISBN 978-0-9957164-9-0 (print)
ISBN 978-0-9957164-8-3 (EPUB)
ISBN 978-0-9957164-7-6 (Kindle)

Cover design by Cecile Richard (cecile-richard.com)
Cover illustration by Jules Scheele (julesscheele.com)
Interior design by Katie West (therealkatiewest.com)

The typefaces used in this publication are Fanwood designed by Barry Schwartz and Myriad Pro designed by Robert Slimbach and Carol Twombly.

Printed in Canada

CONTENTS

INTRODUCTION

It's not an exaggeration to say I owe my whole life to the internet.

Today, I'm an editor. I'm a partner to an amazing person I reconnected with about a Steam game, over Snapchat and the short-lived service Rabb.it. And I spend time with some of my best friends in the world through a series of Power Ranger roleplaying games we've enacted across time zones.

But before all this, I was twelve years old, an only child of divorce, a kid with depression I didn't have the language for yet, and often I felt alone. I spent a lot of my time writing into the absolute vacuums of never-ending Word documents. I didn't know the shape of the person I wanted to be, exactly, but I knew that putting words on the screen would have something to do with it. This was the scene when I started looking for my people on the internet. This was who I was before I realised I could have a second life, one of my making, online.

I joined my first fandom via the Teenage Mutant Ninja Turtles mailing list and the #TMNT IRC channel. (And a lot of other things, probably including Geocities webrings.

I'm dating myself. I remember when it was cool to be able to make "frameless" frames in HTML.)

It opened up the world to me — well, granted, a world of anthropomorphic turtles having sex with human characters in ways that were anatomically questionable, but still. It was a world, and it was one where I could email or chat or, later, MSN-message with people who workshopped my writing and called me on my shit and encouraged me to keep going and sent me care packages of Raphael-centric cartoon episodes on VHS. In this strange new world, I was no longer alone, not even close.

That was the world I grew up in — one where communities online, largely comprised of women, worked together to support, to entertain, to show up for each other. That, to me, was fandom. (In some corners of the internet today, I know it still is.) And that, for me, was the formative experience that made me love writing — and love editing — which has what led me to everything else, including this book.

So many of the pieces of this book speak to the spaces I loved and lived in online. Today, I'm an editor. Back then, I was a beta reader for people I met on the FictionAlley forums. (Fellow passengers on the SS Ron/Hermione: we made it.) I made a lifelong friend across continents on LiveJournal, where I used to be every messy and friends-locked version of myself, relationship drama included. I was catfished there, too, through a friendship I made in an astrology community that carried over onto MSN Messenger. And I met Katie West in real life — but I got to know her on LiveJournal, and later Flickr and Tumblr. Because in that certain era, who you were in real life was just a single Polaroid snap: all the rest, all your most vulnerable and raw and most authentic selves, lived in your words and pictures and art online.

When I was growing up, the internet was the place where you could create yourself into being. Not because you were an artist, necessarily (although many artists of all kinds found the people who would support them online), but because the project that was you was a collaboration that you could work on together with the people you found there. When you wrote into the blinking cursor on that screen, it wasn't the vacuum of a Word document — someone would write back. When you posted that photo, that fanart, that demo, someone commented on it. And those people, whoever they were, whoever they wanted to be, were there because they felt what you felt at the same time you did, no matter where they were and if you'd ever meet.

The truest story of this book is that in the wilder days of the internet, people found a place where they could be anyone — and so they became more truly themselves. They could have met anyone, and while some of them found trolls, catfishers, and attempted predators, some of them met their life partners. Their best friends. Their heart-siblings. And new evolutions of themselves.

I've gone through a whole spectrum of feelings working on this collection. We were so lucky to have the internet as the space we did as we came of age. I can't imagine joining Facebook at twelve, co-existing online with your most embarrassing baby moments, and having all of your receipts — from preteen life on — there for everyone to see and expose. Group chats are great. TikToks can be hilarious. And the meme culture gets me through the day sometimes. But so many of the pieces in this book are about how exploring that relatively anonymous, free-ingly impermanent internet gave people the space to become themselves — to practice themselves into being.

How do you do that now when you're constrained by the need to present only the best version of yourself perpetually from childhood and at all times forever? It's not as if it's easy to opt out of being connected to the internet these days. Where do we go to be ourselves when the internet has made us brands, and the consequences of being human are so dire? And no, that's not a slam on the cancel culture that tells bosses about unapolo-getic bigots — or the internet that rallied to support survivors in #MeToo. But the consequences today's internet offers are double-edged: as brands attached to real names, many people have been able to speak truth to power in ways they never could before. But in the same way — as we saw with Gamer-gate — today's boundary-crash between IRL and the WWW can mean that endless campaigns of harassment become very real and very dangerous. Taking a stance in a YouTube video, in a work you created, in a tweet can lead to almost-ruin. And the growth you might have experienced as a person over years of learning and listening can evaporate in an instant if someone's inclined to dig deep. (Call-outs have become associated with a kind of malice — but once I think they were, and could still be, a form of love, of encouragement to grow.)

I don't know where the freedom to become yourself will be located for future generations. But what I do know is that we can learn from who we were during that time, in that place. What this book shows us is that so many people just want to *talk*. Not in the way that we talk so often IRL, but in that late-night, 3 a.m. way where we rip away our walls to the heart of who we are, and find something in each other that binds us together beyond any connection the bond of sharing space would imply.

This book shows us that people want someone to *care*, to see what it is they're trying to be and trying to accomplish and to acknowledge it and be there for it and uplift it with their praise, with their desire for more, with their constructive criticism.

This book shows us that people across the world, of all ages and from all walks of life, feel the need to be *seen*, not for the meat of their bodies or the number of followers they have, but for the things they love, the things they feel, the ideals they hold so close to their hearts that they could only ever articulate them in the freedom and safety of pseudo-anonymity.

In many ways, I — and Katie and this anthology — have a lot of hope. We hope we can learn how, on today's platforms, with today's "engagement," to give each other the space to talk and be heard, to be cared for, to be seen, to be so thoroughly held and loved, the way we were back then. We hope we can become all those selves we once were again, to hold those selves we meant to be. And we hope we can see who they are, the next generation of explorers, pioneers, creators. We hope we can all find our people again, a whole new second life, better than IRL.

Jasmine Elliot
Editor, *Better Than IRL*
Toronto, January 2020

CONTENT WARNINGS

This book has twenty-three essays covering a vast range of topics from a deep pool of personal experience: from wrestling to roleplay, from dealing with body dysmorphia to dealing with racism, from catfishing to fandoms. We want all our readers to be able to enjoy the experience of reading through this book, so we're including a list of content or trigger warnings for each essay in this anthology.

Our goal at Fiction & Feeling is to elevate underrepresented voices and topics, which can mean that some readers are engaging with topics, experiences, and viewpoints for the first time and may find this strange or uncomfortable. Other readers may find certain topics more difficult to deal with than others. The content of an essay may bring up painful memories or trigger panic attacks. Many topics could potentially be the trigger for such reactions, though there are some main culprits such as abuse, self-harm, violence, blood, war, rape, and eating disorders. Including a content warning at the beginning of a piece of writing that gives a quick description of what can be expected can act as a heads-up for those who need it. Content warnings are not meant to suggest a reader stays away from a piece of writing; rather, they hopefully give a reader some time to prepare themselves for what they're about to encounter. This can be true for either subjects that might cause physical and emotional distress or themes that might be uncomfortable and challenging.

CONTENT WARNINGS

THE PYJARMY

Erica Buist

I'm watching a tear drip down between the floorboards of my bedroom. There it goes. Now here comes another, dripping off my nose. It tickles, but I don't bother to wipe it away. I see dust bunnies under my bed, claiming an old sports bra. My laptop is overheating on the unwashed bedsheets. Inbox: 0. Another wave of humiliation spreads through me. I picture my body gently hitting the floor of a seabed, the sand puffing around me for a moment, and settling.

I reach for my phone, the way an overdosing junkie might in a half-hearted, last-minute decision to call an ambulance. I tilt the screen sideways and open Twitter.

"Turn an internship into a job," I type, slowly, sobs pulsing, "put crack in the boss's coffee. All they'll know is things are just better when you're around."

My cheekbone presses into the wood.

Send tweet.

//

"So, what's this 'blog' you've started?" Tina says, using finger quotes.

"I'm writing it anonymously. It's called How to Be Jobless."

"Which is needed . . . why?" She chuckles to take the sting out of the insult. Tina got hired right after graduation. From the way she's looking at me, you'd think I'd invented 2013's job crisis to annoy her.

"Well," I say evenly, "A million unemployed people should be creating a political earthquake. But we're not, because — there's no *collectivism* among the jobless. We're a million islands. All the advice is based on competing — 'how to stand out,' 'how to take down the competition,' 'how to look good on your bloody *billboard CV.*' Everyone's talking about how doomed the youth are, but no one's talking *to* them, and sure as shit no one's making them laugh."

"So you're planning to make them laugh?" says Tina. I think she believes she's hiding her disdain. Which is awkward, because I can see it. It's like talking to someone who doesn't know their nipple is showing.

"Well," I stammer, "I've done stand-up . . . " I decide to veer away from my blog: "It's weird to think that history students of the future won't be looking at letters or paintings to work out what life was like, isn't it? They'll be looking at tweets and blog posts."

"So that's why you're doing this? So that future historians read your '*blog*'?" Tina drags out the word 'blog' as if for an invisible audience.

"No!" I say, "I was talking about how generally, the internet — "

I stop, because something snaps inside me. It feels good, like the snap of a biscuit, or the pop of a blister containing a tense and shitty friendship. Why am I spending the moments between bouts of shame defending myself against accusations of delusions of grandeur? Why have I spent a chunk of my miniscule weekly budget to be told I'm a useless, deluded wanker? I could have had the same experience at home, with my inbox, for free.

"Sorry, did you invite me to coffee just to bollock me?"

She looks shocked and backtracks, gets very apologetic, but I bat it away and tell her I have to go. On the bus, I pull out my notebook and scribble, "In a society where it's considered rude to answer 'yes' to the question, 'Does anyone want the last scone?' — especially if they're at the next table, I've learned — it's amazing how many people will happily go up to a young job-seeker, pick up their last shred of self-esteem, and dunk it in their tea until it disintegrates into soggy clumps."

I look up from the seabed and see shafts of light. *Yes, Tina*, I think, *I am planning to make them laugh.*

//

"Fuck her!" says Dion, my boyfriend. He's currently exempt from jobhunt hell because he's doing the classic millennial alternative: studying for a master's. At lunchtimes we write joke "tips" to tweet into the listless void, hoping another lonely jobseeker sees them. "She's a troll. You told her you were starting something new, and her first instinct was to tear it down."

"Maybe she's right."

"Maybe she's a troll. Forget her, read me the jokes."

I pull out my notebook.

"*Create an office atmosphere at home by standing up and offering yourself tea thirty-seven times a day.*"

"Funny. Keep."

"*Overworked looking for jobs? Get yourself an unpaid intern. It's both illegal and totally fine.*"

"Keep."

"*Buy a box of Krispy Kremes, smile and say, 'The guys at the office are going to love me!' Haha, you'll think as you eat them over the sink. You win.*"

He chuckles. "That's dark. Keep."

//

There's a dead rat in the alleyway. That doesn't feel like a good sign. But a bird shitting on your head supposedly brings luck, so perhaps a dead rat outside your new office is also, in some way, positive?

At 4 p.m. on Friday, a harried editor at a website trying to be BuzzFeed called and offered me a weeklong "job trial." The job pays £16,000 a year — which he apologetically acknowledged is impossible to live on in London.

But it's a shot.

A little man greets me, "Hi, are you here for work experience?"

I deflate, picture shaking him by the lapels, growling, "No, I'm here for a *job*. I have a deadline. I have entered 'KILL SELF' into my calendar one year from now, and while I'm 98% sure I'm joking, I am definitely *not* here for 'work experience,' because I'm not your fifteen-year-old niece."

Instead, I give a wobbly, "Yes."

I spend the week doing my best to impress Little Man and Harried Editor. Two of my pieces are very popular; one is even plagiarised by a bigger, more successful site.

On my last day, a Gmail notification pops up. It's from Harried. I catch, "We'll get the contract sent over to you later today" before it disappears. When I open my emails, it isn't there. I refresh. Nothing. I ask Harried if he can resend the email.

"I didn't email you," he says, confused.

"Something about a contract?"

He looks down and mutters incomprehensibly. Little springs to action, as if Harried just yelled, "Clean up on aisle five!" He crouches over my computer, "Ah, I think last week's intern has her Gmail set up on this computer, hang on, let me just take that off . . . "

The realisation pours over me, slowly and heavily, like treacle from a bucket. They already hired someone, but they couldn't start this week. That's why the call was so last minute. I'm here to plug the gap with free work, under the guise of being "on trial," of having a shot.

At 5 p.m. I leave politely, wishing everyone a nice weekend. I walk past the dead rat, which after five days of being scavenged is little more than a stain on the pavement. When I get on the tube, fat tears of embarrassment roll down my face.

I pull out my phone.

I tweet: "It's Friday! Go to a bar and join in with someone's work drinks, then watch as they pretend to remember that time you met at the water cooler."

//

The message comes as I'm Googling "how to delete a blog": "Hello, your Twitter made me snort. I'd LOVE to talk to you for a feature for GoThinkBig." I agree to write "The Definitive Guide to How to Be Jobless" for the careers-focused website for young people, after which the editor offers me a column, "My Week in Joblessness."

It feels like grabbing onto the fin of a dolphin. And I know just where to start.

How to Survive a Job "Trial" From Someone Who Probably Didn't

Happy Friday, pyjama'd and pyjama-bound people. I'm very excited to now be a regular contributor to GoThinkBig. I'm rarely even a regular contributor to my own outfits (roll around in a pile of laundry long enough and you'll find yourself dressed. Quite a stress saver).

I'll kick off with my experience of a new type of job interview. Do as I didn't, jobseekers.

Some journalism employers have realised a high-pressure twenty-minute interview is largely useless for finding out whether a candidate can come up with ideas, write, get on with co-workers, and meet deadlines. Hence the new type of interview: The Trial. Get the applicant in for a week of free work: the employer finds out what they need to know, and the candidate gets all the awkwardness of an interview with the added excruciation of the first week in a new office.

What fun it must be to watch them pray, "Don't screw up, don't screw up…"

Here's how I did.

You don't have the job yet

The problem with The Trial is it has the same name as the period after you've been hired and they're double-checking that you're not a smelly weirdo with odd socks and a ferret stuffed down your shirt. The time when they reserve the right to say, "We've made a ghastly error, you most definitely do not have the job, please vacate the premises and take your ferret with you."

A trial isn't "the job is yours unless you're Creepy Ferret Boy." It's an extended interview. So turn up on time and behave like someone they'd want to see every day.

How I ballsed this up: I got way too excited. For a fleeting moment, I thought I had a job, or at least a reasonable shot at one.

The senior writer welcomed me at the door with a question that brought me back to earth and my actual position on it: "Hi, are you here for work experience?"

Oh. I was not nearly a staff writer. I was not a big achiever who leapt off the page. I was not the proverbial shit. They were trialling other people, and this was not a job offer pending ferret concerns.

You're SO not one of the gang yet

Inside jokes whizz around you like Dementors. If you attempt to join in with a conversation there's a half-second pause in which they stare at you as if you've just said, "Guys, look at this rash on the inside of my cheek! Look by TOUCHING!"

They're not trying to be cold. They're a close-knit team, they've probably worked through a lot of awkwardness to get where they are. You haven't put those hours in yet.

How I ballsed this up: I got in on a game of foosball (it's one of those offices). I don't know why I expected laughter and high-fives. We didn't even make eye contact — I honestly couldn't pick any of them out of a line-up.

Also, I sucked. Whenever my teammate scored, the girl opposite me said, "Good shot, Elizabeth."

"Well-played, Elizabeth."

"You're beating us now — *Elizabeth.*"

Eating lunch together — don't freak out

Lunch is an opportunity to hang out and show how great you are.
How I ballsed this up: The team invited me to have sushi with them.
Unfortunately, I'm allergic to shellfish. Even the smell makes me feel
ill and, in especially embarrassing circumstances, closes my throat.
Instead of explaining this properly, I said, "I can't, when I go into sushi
restaurants I die. I mean I vomit. I vomit from shellfish. I vomit from
the smell. I mean I gag. Not vomit, necessarily. Oh god, I'm sorry I keep
saying vomit. Enjoy your lunch."

Dress well

You'd think this goes without saying.
How I ballsed this up: On my last day, a good hour and a half after I got
in, I noticed there was a stain on my top. How did this happen? Did I roll
around in the wrong pile of clothes? How could my system fail me?
I scrabbled for some brilliant reason I could give for looking like I'd
eaten porridge lying down, on a rollercoaster, drunk.
I know — I'll say I saw a friend at the bus stop, and kindly held her baby
while she tied her shoelace, and the dribbly bundle of joy spit up on me.
But how was I going to mention that casually across a near-silent
office? I couldn't stand up and announce, "Look, everyone! Hear ye,
hear ye! Feast your eyes upon what a BABY did to my top, fresh from
the clean pile of clothes by my bed, NOT the dirty pile by my door!"
I kept quiet. Probably the smartest thing I did all week.
They said they'd let me know.

//

The column draws people in, and fast. They start tweeting
at me, sharing their joblessness woes, thanking me for making
them laugh. In one exchange, a man refers to the jobless as the
"pyjama army," which becomes the hashtag #Pyjarmy.

Hence my eighth column:

A Letter From the Jobless Trenches

Dear Family,

It's my 159th day in the jobless trenches. Sorry I haven't written in a while. I've been busy in my cycle of applying for jobs and listening to crickets. Thanks for the socks and biscuits. I've eaten them.

Sorry my first letter was so self-pitying. I admit a funeral playlist was a tad dramatic, and the Coldplay closer unforgivable. The jobless trenches are rough. Maybe I'm being punished for the times I over-pronounced French words.

Still, don't despair for me, family, it's comfy enough — the jobless trenches are built out of pillows and blankets. So we don't get trench-foot. We get application-arse.

This is how we live, hidden from sight in the troughs of unemployment, our self-esteem so low we address our covering letters, "To whom it probably doesn't concern."

Sometimes we pop our heads over the top and stare over at The Other Trench — the one for The Employed. We hear about it from our comrades who made it over. Tales of leather chairs, fridges with labelled leftovers, bunkers of instant coffee, pet unicorns, glitter (ruins the coffee, but makes their tongues look like disco balls, so they say).

I tell them hope is a dangerous thing. It's got no use in the trough.

At night come the screams: "WHY haven't they replied? It's been THREE MONTHS! I'm PERFECT for it, you SADISTS!"

I feel most sorry for Tommy. Every few days, he speculatively pops his head over the top and yells to The Other Trench, "I am shouting to apply for the position of — " BANG. He gets shot with one of their "NO" bullets, every time. But he keeps trying.

Despite being "all in this together," the sad fact is we're competitors. We go over the top, and slowly, we march, in our hundreds of thousands, towards the few job vacancies in The Other Trench, most of us cannon fodder for the monsoon of "NO" bullets, of which they seem to have a limitless supply.

Saddest to know is that this, so far, is our generation's greatest fight — wincing and marching on, hoping the bullets will miss us, hoping we'll get through, hoping to taste that glittery coffee.

//

The #pyjarmy hashtag trickles steadily into my timeline: "Today I got dressed," one follower tweets. "Am I a traitor to the #pyjarmy?!"

"I found the @howtobejobless blog!" one person tweets at her friend. "I'm now giggling happily."

"Glad to be of service darling," she replies. "Welcome to the #pyjarmy! *Salute*"

Recruiters start using it. "Oi oi #pyjarmy — could YOU be our next Team Assistant?"

When people get in touch, I tweet, "Soldiers! We have a new recruit in the jobless trenches. Make them feel welcome. As you were." When one follower gets hired, she tweets, "Right, #pyjarmy, I'm demobbing for a runner job at Sky. Back in three months, will bring supplies!"

"First 'sorry your application has not been successful' email since quitting my job," tweets another. "This is going to be an uphill struggle . . . this time around I'll have the Pyjarmy for moral support."

"You certainly will," I reply. "Chin up, soldier!"

"Hold fast, you'll get there," someone else replies.

I sit on my bed and watch the replies of support. I can't believe it.

It's working.

//

As I approach the looming Guardian offices, I am certain of just one thing: I am an imposter. I only hoped to get far enough to screw it up for blog fodder — but now, positivity is slithering in like a leech. I rush writing up my column, to squash any hope that it had gone well.

An Interview at the Guardian: Expectations vs. Reality

In the last week of August, the universe decided I wasn't so bad after all and threw me a bone. Two, in fact. In my largely bone-free existence, this was a boney landslide.

The first was thrown by a batty family member. He'd bought a car and was driving to the Loire Valley to celebrate. Taking pity on me after I spent my life savings on a journalism master's only to become the poster child for unemployment, he offered to take me along and stuff me with cheese. A holiday in France! Magnifique!

The second bone was thrown by the Guardian. The email came while I was packing. It read, roughly:

Dear HTBJ,

We are delighted to invite you to an assessment centre for the Guardian Digital Journalism Scheme. Your appointment will be early in the morning in the middle of the only holiday you're likely to have in, quite literally, years. The mid-week train back to London will cost over £100 and there's a MASSIVE chance we'll reject you anyway, since you have a knack for messing up these sorts of opportunities.

We look forward to meeting you, as chances are you'll make some excellent blunder we'll dine out on for years.
Lol,
the Guardian

Okay, I didn't exactly copy-paste that, but it's an accurate representation of what I saw. Inconvenient? Absolutely. But it was a bone. A delicious, much-needed bone. Here's what it was like to frantically gnaw on it.

Arriving at the Guardian offices

Expectation: The receptionist will say, "Ah yes, here you are, under 'jobless oddball invited in error.'" Then she'll press a button and the trap door I'll be conveniently standing on will open, and I'll disappear with an echoey "Nooooooo!"
Reality: I must have been standing to the left of the trap door because she gave me a visitor's badge and told me to take a seat.
The chairs were the kind that situate your arse well below your knees, so I spent the twenty-minute wait hoping I'd be able to get out of it without ending up as a BuzzFeed GIF.

The dress code

Expectation: The Guardian's lefty and cool, so people won't be too smart. They'll be dressed similar to me — Doc Martens, casual tops, at least one hole in everyone's trousers.
Reality: Nope. Impeccable suits, high heels, and brushed hair. I bet they used an actual mirror to get ready. I panicked — but it's the Guardian! Last week it was reported that a smackhead had been wandering in to shoot up in their bathrooms, for goodness' sake!
I calmed down somewhat to note that while the candidates were smartly dressed and reading the paper, the employees walking in

looked more like me — each casually dressed, tapping digital devices, sucking at the teat of a Pret coffee cup like a shuddering addict.

Then it hit me — Doc Martens. Boots used in the 70s by skinheads to kick minorities to death. And I was wearing them at the Guardian. They had red ribbon laces, but still.

I was done for.

The exercises

Expectation: We were told in the invitation email that there would be a subbing test, a writing exercise, and a group task. I hoped it would be a trust exercise where you catch someone falling backwards off a ledge. Then if we dropped someone and they got concussed, there'd be one less interviewee in the running.

Reality: The group exercise had an extremely low concussion risk. We sat in a semi-circle and discussed how to digitally present three news stories. The editorial team perched themselves in a line and took reams of notes, as if observing the contents of an aquarium. It was all I could do not to make a fish face and forget everything after three seconds. One candidate suggested the way to digitally feature news of the *Fifty Shades of Grey* casting was to have the general public upload their own speculative audition tapes. I heard myself say, "That might be quite frightening."

I'm sure one of them wrote, "The one who waltzed in from France wearing racist boots fears non-traditional sex. NGM (not Guardian material)."

The next stage

Expectation: They told us they were going to "discuss the candidates" (read: "exterminate twenty-three from the list"). The remaining twelve will have an hour-long interview with the editor-in-chief.

I'm sure they'll let us know on Tuesday afternoon, as promised.

They know we're terrified of either outcome — a nerve-crunching sixty minutes trying to impress Alan Rusbridger, or yet another soul-soddening rejection.

They'll definitely get a move on, so as not to leave us dangling like hogs over a spit roast yet to be lit.

Reality: Nope. Still haven't heard. The suspense burns. My heart breakdances every time I hear an email ping, and my smackhead-in-the-toilets routine hasn't made me as privy to the right gossip as you'd think.

If they find out my little bag of heroin is actually nutmeg, I'm finished.

My aim, to squash the positivity leech, is once again messed up by the support of the avatars. Because the column goes viral.

People tweet at the Guardian that they "have to" hire me, rush to alert me to a Guardian editor encouraging "whoever wrote that piece" to get in touch to be commissioned. I'm swimming right under the surface, shafts of light dancing across my face as I'm buoyed by the encouragement and support of people who don't even know my name.

I walk into the final interview feeling the furthest thing from isolation, the opposite of loneliness.

//

"So it's an internship?" says my friend.

"No, it's a job."

"How long is the contract?"

"A year."

"Is it paid?"

"Yes."

"Wow, a *paid* internship!"

"It's a job."

"Amazing, well done! Honestly, back at uni, I never thought we'd get anywhere."

I say nothing, because wow.

"And now you're an intern at the Guardian!"

"It's not an . . . " I sigh. Why did I tell my flesh friends before my avatar friends? "Thanks."

//

I tell the avatars. For two days, I'm buried in messages.

"The #Pyjarmy commander @howtobejobless has gone and got herself a job at the Guardian! Congrats and thanks for all the help!"

"So chuffed that @howtobejobless got a dream journo job! Her blog brought laughter and empathy to media job hunters everywhere!"

"She's been an inspiration to all aspiring journos to not give up!"

"I love @howtobejobless and so happy for her! She's helped a lot of us, the Guardian are very lucky!"

"AMAZING news. Yours is an inspiring story for anyone facing a grisly rejection letter today."

"I rarely root for others to succeed (it's a character flaw) but really hoped you'd get that job. Congrats!"

"YES! It's like when a sitcom ends in a way you want it to."

"Big congratulations. Do visit us in the trenches and bring fresh doughnuts."

And among the deluge is a message from Tina.

It reads, simply, "You're an inspiration."

//

It is strange to be thanked by the people who saved you. I don't know how to explain the isolation I felt before the Pyjarmy, how their solidarity brought me to the surface. So I said goodbye the only way I could, still anonymous to all but those few obsessed with solving the mystery.

The only thing that really gets you through something as sloggingly depressing as unemployment is the support of other people. They don't have to be people you've met, and the support doesn't have to be in hug form. Find and hook whoever makes you laugh, whatever stops you turning into a self-absorbed crinkle-faced whingey-pants bore. And that's what I did. So thank you, guys.

You got me through.

I'M FROM THE INTERNET;
WHERE ARE *YOU* FROM?

Mimi Mondal

Where are you from? is the question you build your life around when you're a small brown woman in a Western country. I heard it after stepping out of India and moving to a small campus in Scotland, and I heard it after moving to the US two years later, but by that time, I was already used to it. I had been answering that question for a decade, though I hadn't lived anywhere outside Calcutta for the first twenty-five years of my life.

Where are you from? — I was just a kid from the next street. *Where are you from?* — Nobody in my family looked or sounded like me. *Why do you look like that?* — Nobody at school wore all black through the sweltering summers of Calcutta or pierced holes in their face and stuck bits of shiny metal in them. *Where do you even get those ideas?* — No other teenager read books or listened to music that no one else had heard of. I consumed images that didn't exist in the mainstream media in India back in the early-and-mid-2000s, subcultures that nobody had heard of, at least not anyone from backgrounds like mine: barely middle-class people, first generation in the city, with nobody in the family who had ever been or knew anyone from abroad.

The answer, which sounded unimaginable back then and sounds sassy even now if I don't unpack it, remains simple: I am from The Internet. I was one of the earliest generation of internet natives — teenagers who found themselves online in the early 2000s, formed friendships and cultural exchanges and, eventually, entire communities that couldn't have existed in an earlier generation — and so far off the Western centres of that phenomenon, I was relatively rare.

I wasn't the only one of my kind, of course. But India is a large, overcrowded country, so the experience of being "few and far between" takes a different shape altogether. It isn't the same experience as being the only kid on the internet in a small town in the heartlands of America — someone who grew up different from everyone else when "everyone else" was a few thousand people who all knew each other.

In Calcutta, a city of over fourteen million people in one of the most densely populated regions in the world, being "weird" isn't a lonely experience. Being weird in Calcutta is being eyeballed by a few thousand people every day as you jostle them on public transport, as you're pitted against them at school and in tuition classes while your parents drive to turn you all into a vast wave of doctors and engineers, as you balance between retaining your culture and being sufficiently Westernised to be employable.

Calcutta is an old colonial city — its riverside location, its old buildings with their colonnades and sprawling porticos, its elite private clubs, and above all its culture, all still reverentially preserving the echoes of London. But that imprint is from an older era of Westernisation, the access to it belonging to a different social class and caste than my family. My parents couldn't afford a membership to one of the private clubs of Calcutta, but they could afford a dial-up internet connection for Rs. 250 a month.

//

I had not always been the kid that stood out from the crowd. But in 2000, just about when I turned thirteen, my father enrolled me in a computer literacy summer course, solely because someone had told him that computers were the latest booming market for jobs. (Learning to use them was something akin to typing skills for a previous generation, he assumed.) My school didn't yet offer a computer class, and my father wanted me to be ahead of the curve of the 500-odd classmates who'd all inevitably want those precious jobs a few years on.

I remember the lessons from that class: MS Office (Word, Excel, PowerPoint), Internet Explorer, email, and chat. I came out of it with my first Yahoo! email ID and a revelation about Yahoo! chatrooms. I spent the next few months obsessively online at my neighbourhood cyber café — more and more hours every day — and explaining to my parents that it was necessary for school.

In 2001 I got my first computer, assembled with parts pur-chased from the black market and put together by an engineer my father hired, loaded with pirated editions of Windows 95 and MS Office. Still, I was the only one among my friends to have a computer at home and all to myself, since my parents didn't understand how it worked. That PC lasted my family over a decade, resembling quite the Ship of Theseus by the time it was junked in 2015.

It was on that PC that I constructed from scratch the person I am today.

//

Other people have written more eloquently than me about the inventiveness of the poor, the desperate workaholism of the immigrant, and the way some of us have to learn to code-switch and adapt to changing environments from childhood, to the point that those things become as effortless as breathing by the time we're adults.

My mother's family arrived in Calcutta in the mid-1960s, in a wave of refugees from what was then East Pakistan (and is now Bangladesh). My father's family didn't start arriving until the early 1980s, though they had to travel a shorter distance — some 130 kilometres from a village in the district of Medinipore. The socio-cultural distance was far more immense than these geographies suggest. Both my parents' families were from castes that are now commonly known as Dalit, though the word "untouchable" still circulates. The eastern part of India is relatively more liberal than the rest, so there's no experience of actual untouchability in my family's recorded memory, but there has always been social segregation, often unspoken, couched in civility and dog-whistle terms.

My parents, uncles, and aunts went to college and got their jobs through the affirmative action initiatives of the government (more commonly known as "quotas"), but promotions and benefits always arrived late, colleagues and neighbours didn't often make the effort to go beyond polite acquaintance, and grown sons and daughters weren't accepted in marriage into families outside our castes. To all outside appearance we were just like other city people — an appearance we tried our best to maintain — but we were always this parallel community, unrepresented in history, people who didn't even know our own pasts beyond a generation or two. My family didn't know many things that other city people took for granted and usually didn't know anyone they could ask.

In 1986 my mother received a small electric baking oven as a wedding gift. It hadn't come with a manual, and she didn't learn to use it until twenty-five years later. All my growing-up years, I saw that oven packed away in a storage shelf in our house — this alien device a tangible proof of how much we didn't belong, how much we needed to keep pretending that we did.

Looking back from the distance of almost two decades, I realise we were people who had so little, knew so little, were allowed into so few spaces. (I didn't feel so impoverished back then, because my family had come from even less. My parents were doing better than the relatives who never made it out of the village. I was learning more things than second and third cousins who weren't even sent to school. I was still far enough down from the glass ceiling to be able to look up and see only the sky.)

Then, at the turn of the century, I went online.

//

What the internet did for me, though at thirteen I was too young to understand all of it, was to first introduce me to those privileged social circles in Calcutta into which my parents could never enter — and then propel me further, much further into the whole wide world. India is a country where coded social markers have always been rigid, closely monitored, and nearly insurmountable. Access to Westernisation is itself a class marker; whether a child was a rebellious goth or a well-mannered Jane Austen lover was less significant than the fact that they both signalled their family's ability to immerse them in Western culture. I didn't know it at the time, but when I let the internet transform me — devouring books and media that weren't available in the market in India, much of it pirated; befriending people elsewhere in the world and rapidly code-switching to emulate their distant subcultures — I was also erasing from my real-life body the barely urban, Dalit markers of my family.

Online was where I also made my local friends. We bonded over shared interests, often subcultural interests that weren't common in India at the time, ranging everywhere from rock music, Hollywood movies, science fiction, and fandom to conversations about gender, sexuality, body modification, or mental health. Not every one of those friends had to make as much of a social leap as I did to blend into that environment; many of them did come from families with sufficient Western immersion. But the internet was where those boundaries from real life disappeared, where I was *allowed* to write the bio that felt truest to myself, choose my username, consume any media I wanted, and change myself any way I wanted.

It made us such an incredibly different generation from our parents, even in our IRL interactions. Suddenly I could be hanging out with another teen who didn't go to the same school as me, whose family would never socialise with mine, but the part of our identities that really mattered was the bands we both loved whose music we had downloaded from torrents. In Calcutta in the 2000s, we internet-literate teens were a subculture of our own, unlike the larger majority of our school friends who were still part of the old social order.

Not all of us were into the same things. What really made us similar was internet culture, with its endless freedom to choose who you wanted to be — so very different from the way we were raised. Individuality was not considered a desirable quality in India at any social level; both the privileged and the marginalised were expected to stay within their limits, enjoy the small range of sanctimonious media that was officially available in our country (looking at Bollywood here!), and grow up to live exactly like our parents. What brought me and my friends together at that age was that we were all subversive and rebellious, though we might have been rebelling about different things. And all of us were extremely online.

In that disparate group of internet-literate teens, everyone was the tip of a *very different* iceberg, unlike our other school-uniform-wearing, syllabus-book-reading, Bollywood-cinema-watching peers. Some of my local friends were metalheads. A small subset of that circle listened to punk rock, but I was the only one in the group who leaned towards goth — I was the only goth anyone knew. All of our music came from the internet. My first boyfriend was a dedicated rapper, and the local hip hop "scene" was just him. I hung out a lot on body modification websites and forums, with many hours spent on BMEzine. The bravest of us went to local tattoo artists and piercers with guidelines found online, allowing them to work on our bodies with absolutely no expertise. We couldn't get brands like Hot Topic or Manic Panic to deliver in India in the 2000s, but we were tuned to the aesthetic, emulating it the best we could with local products. Some of our interests were less public than the others — like the LGBTQ forums I inhabited for years before I started looking for local queer friendships, or that one friend who worked as a cam girl, but never disclosed it in her real-life circles.

Where are you from? The same cramped, poorly renovated house in the same refugee-resettlement neighbourhood, which wouldn't get gentrified and cooler for another decade. Through all those years, my get-home curfew was a strict 8 p.m., because the streets outside would get unsafe past then. My family never went on a vacation, even inside India, though my father commuted long, backbreaking hours for his job — travelling for pleasure was never affordable. But I switched on that PC, hit the dial-up, demanded nobody made a phone call, and my assembled PC became my window to the world in a world that offered me very few windows.

//

All the IRL friendships of my late teens were forged online. It became hard to connect with people who didn't exist on the internet, even if we met them in our social circles. It was as if a whole dimension of their personalities was missing, and they too perceived us only on the surface, which was very little of who we truly were. Orkut was where we made new local friends. I got to know my first boyfriend through his Blogger blog, where he put up his music, though we had been introduced by friends in person.

Blogger was also where I became a writer — I wrote a popular poetry blog for a few years. I was also publishing in some local venues, but print publications for young writers were rare and poorly circulated, and that traditional publication credit in an obscure print magazine or anthology disappeared faster than it took to achieve it. Because of that blog, my peers knew me to be a poet, and their enthusiastic comments kept me wanting to write and improve, though nobody in my family read or cared for what I was writing.

What really changed my life in a permanent way were the fandom communities of LiveJournal and later Dreamwidth and Archive of Our Own. Science fiction and fantasy books were rare in India in my teens. Bookstores and libraries carried a small shelf of mainly old classics, their ownership gate-kept by clusters of "respectable" men. Fandom was almost a secret hobby for me and others like me: the girls, the queer and non-binary people, the weirdoes, all of whom found our corners of fandom, away from the guys who claimed we would never understand the "true depth" of the works of Asimov or Tolkien.

We were the kids of the *Harry Potter* boom — a global phenomenon on a scale that was only possible in those years when the internet was rapidly spreading beyond Western countries. In *Harry Potter* fanfiction communities and others that branched out from them, we met nerds who talked to us and made us feel welcome, helped us continue being nerds in the face of those guys' scorn and open hostility. In those online communities we also learned to be *better* nerds than those guys, because we were participating in contemporary conversations, learning new things, reading other people's stories, and receiving feedback on ours.

Several of my current colleagues in the Indian science fiction and fantasy community were teenagers I met online in those years. Nearly all of us would've stopped pursuing those interests if we didn't find those online communities and find each other within them. While we participated in the big Western fandoms like *Harry Potter*, *Lord of the Rings*, or *Star Wars*, we also wrote local fanfiction as well as original stories for each other. Every year during the Kaleidoscope holiday fic exchange for the dark_agenda community on LiveJournal (later also on Dreamwidth and AO3), which focused on fandoms of colour, some of us found a corner to request and write subversive stories based on the Ramayana or the Mahabharata, Bollywood films we liked, or not-strictly-SFF novels published from India that the rest of the global fandom wasn't reading. Those communities were where we cut our teeth in writing, reviewing, debating, and speculating, as well as where we learned to be friends with each other. They were where we discovered, reinforced, and shared an SFF sensibility that was uniquely *from* India, a journey that was not quite the same as that of Indian teens who grew up in the West.

Many of us have grown up to be SFF writers, journalists, and reviewers or scholars of SFF, media, digital humanities, and other related subjects. In India, where SFF is still not a large-scale industry, some of us dropped out and branched into other professions as we grew up, but as adults we keep running into each other. A new book here, a perceptive review there, an event invitation, a PhD dissertation, or indie film of interest, and it turns out we had hung out with that person a decade ago on some fandom forum. Nearly all of us are the same age — a localised generation of our own, not entirely like our friends who grew up in the West, but also not like the people our age in India who didn't get online at the same time.

//

I talk a lot about the internet, even when I'm not "talking about the internet." I talk about the internet when I talk about postcolonialism, Dalitness, immigration, gender, sexuality, academia, fandom, writing fiction, mental health — it's almost a separate intersection of my personality, omnipresent and intertwined with everything else.

Adults like me are no longer rare. We're older millennials, part of that internet-watershed generation, teenagers who had once jumped into this new medium with our boundless naïve optimism and no roadmap to navigate it passed down from our parents.

In some ways, internet culture as a whole reflects the age and maturity timeline of our generation. Some of our parents and grandparents followed us online, but *they* never became part of internet culture the same way. The map of the internet didn't change on a large scale to accommodate them. Their only imprint on the internet remains the awkward, occasionally hilarious ineptitude at navigating a world they don't quite understand. We learned to use filters when our uncomfortable older relatives added us on Facebook. We disappeared behind usernames and restricted profiles. We shifted our conversations to other platforms they didn't know. The internet was never an equal playing field for the previous generation to catch up with us.

When I was younger, the internet felt like an unmistakably young place — no parents around to watch us, and the only older people you would meet were either vaguely awkward or vaguely creepy, trying to hang out in communities younger than themselves. It's a different experience for the waves of younger people who are arriving on the internet today, often introduced to it by their parents who have already shared their youths online.

These days I love the internet like one loves an old friend — both of us somewhat past our youngest days, somewhat deflated from that massive rush of optimism that propelled us before we knew worse, mistakes made and learned from, hopefully stronger and wiser for every wrinkle and grey hair we have to show, trying to make things better for the kids. It's the camaraderie of decades of shared experience that probably exists only between contemporaries.

The internet grew up with us. It's not that there weren't predators lurking online a decade or longer ago, but the scale of unsavoury encounters usually felt proportionate to our own age and maturity, for our predators were learning the scope of the internet at the same pace as us. On occasion, we were the ones who shared inadvisable content — politically incorrect thoughts, photos that left us vulnerable to harm — but we had a relatively wider berth to get rid of them before their consequences caught up with us. On a larger, more watchful internet teeming with a wide and diverse population of adults who actually know how to use it, younger people today have a much narrower groove laid out for them.

Or maybe they don't; maybe they're building and adapting the internet in ways that will be unrecognisable to us in another decade's time. A striking thing about the internet as we know it is precisely its contemporaneity. Think of anyone: from developer-entrepreneurs like Mark Zuckerberg of Facebook, Larry Page and Sergei Brin of Google, Jack Dorsey of Twitter, and Brad Fitzpatrick of LiveJournal; to hackers and whistleblowers like Julian Assange, Chelsea Manning, and Aaron Schwartz; to survivors of major online hate campaigns like Zoë Quinn and Anita Sarkeesian — it's hard to find a name that has significantly influenced the internet culture of our generation who happens to be under thirty or over fifty. All our heroes and villains of the internet belong to our own generation. There's no reason why the next generation should merely inherit the roadmaps that we pass down to them.

//

In the parts of the internet that I inhabit these days, the discussions range from politics, ethics, and identity to climate change, net neutrality, intellectual property rights, privacy, surveillance, and many futurisms. I have grown to be a very different adult from my parents, so much that even during our most convivial conversations, few of my intellectual concerns make sense to them, and hardly any advice they have to offer applies to the circumstances in my life.

Will the next generation of internet natives be just as incomprehensible to me? Will there be a day I won't even understand their systems or language, all the challenges and dilemmas that will affect their lives in very real ways, but won't sound like anything but gibberish to me? As an SFF writer, I am acutely aware of the eventual impossibility of foreseeing the future. The future will always surprise you in unexpected ways. But if everything was already predictable, where would be the fun?

And after all, I survived. Most of our generation survived plunging headfirst into the rush of unknown technology and communities of strangers, abandoning the familiar patterns of our parents, turning ourselves into the kinds of people no one could imagine before. We came out of it with a few scars, but so many stories to tell. Some of those stories are dark, and they have a disconcerting number of adherents, but the generosity of strangers on the internet keeps failing to run out, much to my own immense surprise and delight.

If there is one thing I hope remains constant in the internet of the future, it is that well-spring of generosity and sharing. That saved my life when I was young, and I hope everyone who comes to the internet in the future finds in it a bigger, kinder world and a more enriched way of living. Their internet may be completely unrecognisable from mine, and any advice I have to share may become obsolete and irrelevant, but they will make their own world and survive it, I'm sure. We did.

3 A.M.

Damien Patrick Williams

Ever since I was a kid, well before the world wide web version of the internet was a thing, my dad would wake me up at one or two in the morning, we would wander around the city I was born in, and I would get to see the world in a different way. We walked through the neighbourhood taking in all it had to offer — late-night takeout; conversations with people you'd otherwise never get to meet or talk to; a convenience store or major city artery, known for being clogged with people and traffic, now empty. It was a time of connection, of possibilities, of potential, of getting to know the world in a whole new way; a time when anything might happen, because nothing and everything did. The same street hustle busy-ness of a major city, but quieter, closer, more intense — like everybody who was awake knew what it meant to be up and out and moving at that time. Even when I didn't know that was what I was feeling, it was a magical time and space, a liminal, interstitial, in-between kind of life. I've been drawn to that space between worlds for most of my life. Three a.m. has always been a time for magic.

A ritual space is any of those times and places which we set as special and apart, either through mentality, mood, or meaning. In sociology and trauma studies, "safe spaces" are ritual spaces; in martial arts, the dojo; in traditional Western systems of magic, the drawing of the circle. To mark out the ritual space, we use a knife, or chalk, or a song, or our words, or the movements of our bodies, and we carve out something sacred from within the profane, something astonishing out of, through, *because of* the mundane. A magical place is often felt as atemporal, liminal, no-time and no-place connecting everywhere and everywhere, all at once. The internet of the early 2000s was perfectly this: a combination of the everyday seen through the lens of the wondrous. Everything we did there was a minor miracle, and every connection, a live wire. By the time the internet and I found each other, it was like sparks jumping, like a switch getting thrown. Almost immediately, I felt what the internet could do and be and mean for me. Because on the internet, especially in its early days, it was always 3 a.m. somewhere.

We moved from my hometown right before I turned thirteen, and I got deeply upset about being taken away from the people and places I knew. While there's always the promise that you'll keep in touch, a 700-mile gulf, for teenagers, might as well be opposite ends of the world. I'm not the first person to move away from home right at the edge of the turmoil that is high school, but I have to believe it was a different quality of thing for those of us whose living through that came right at the same time as the whole wide world finding the internet. A breakage with the physical, at the exact moment of being opened up to the digital; a rawness and displacement in our hearts and selves, right when we could share that rough-edged vulnerability with people anywhere in the world. Right when we needed to connect the most, "connection" took on a whole new meaning.

The internet was a new way of understanding life and the world, moving into and through high school and on into college, and part of me wonders, even now, what it would have been like to have experienced these things with the people I'd grown up with. What would I have learned, and who would I have become if I hadn't been open and searching, in exactly that way, right at that time? Would I have been willing to take the risks and feel out the things I did? To search for just the right screennames on AIM and Yahoo!; to find my nicks and log on to IRC (Internet Relay Chat), day after day, to talk about magick; or to eventually build a loving and trusting community, on LiveJournal? And if I hadn't done any of those things, who would I be now?

Throughout the late 90s and early 2000s, as the BBSes and other message boards gave up ground to AOL and AIM and Yahoo!, these new forms and places felt full of strange potential — like despite their corporate origins, they held the possibility of becoming anything at all. The paths I took online took this possibility and transformed online spaces into magical places — IRC rooms became covens and circles and vectors for experimentation and exploration, and places like LiveJournal iterated new ways of creating and building and bonding. This era of the internet was where I and many others discovered how the chance encountering of the right word or phrase at just the right moment might weave together connections that could last whole lifetimes. Where you could meet the people you would give your whole heart to, dozens of times over. Online life gave us access to people and experiences we otherwise never could have known. Experiences made manifest as interlocking enchantments built out of a particular AIM screenname coming online at just the right time of night, or the spells worked by the rotating cast of a relay chat channel, or the hidden mysteries of the comments in a friends-locked LiveJournal post. So very many of us were shaped and made by this pervasively atemporal place in time — when life on the internet was about this need, this desire, this vulnerability, and this wonder at the possibilities available in this interlacing threshold between electricity, spirit, and flesh.

On LiveJournal, it was always 3 a.m. Every post was an open confessional box, every comment thread a space for soul-bare conversations undimmed by time zones, and every community an opportunity to forge friendships and families in which you could share anything, always. That's not to say that LJ as a whole was some perfect land where everything was beautiful and nothing hurt, but rather that it was a space where we could take our time, cultivate our connections, take chances with our openness and vulnerability, and bring together groups of people we were proud to know and trust. This was a space and a place in time where we could take the exceedingly intimate practice of journaling and combine it with something like writing a letter to someone we loved, and each expression and voice was the writer's own. It wasn't just that we felt like we had to do that, but that we felt like we *could* do that that made LiveJournal embody that feeling of ritual space.

My early LJ days were filled with stream-of-consciousness rants that danced between incoherent and deeply emotionally open expressions of joy and rage and frustrations and wonderment. Cutting a hole in the veil of the self and letting people in only matters if you're giving them everything you can about yourself — confession only works if you're honest. Sacrifice only works if it means something. My posts were simultaneously meeting halls and ritual spaces, and the offerings to be made in them. Vital slices of self by which pacts of trust and mutual support were sealed. *Welcome to Nightvale* has since said that if you tell someone a dangerous secret, you give them the power to destroy you, and that this, in fact, is what love is. But long before this, many of us understood the power in whispering shared vulnerabilities in the dark with those we care about, giving each the power to destroy the other. This, for so many of us, was exactly what love was. The magic I learned, back then, was the power of creating, accepting, inhabiting, sharing the space to be vulnerable, the space to break open something sealed and hidden, the space to move in the world in a way that was otherwise unknown. Across every open window and every new post, a room in a temple, a clearing in a moonlit forest, that we made for and with each other.

I was lucky, in so many ways. I mean, so many of us were, back then. First and foremost, we had access to this event, this phenomenon that was online life, in this one precise span of moments; that alone is a massive advantage, and one which allowed us to be and think in all these new ways. We were the first ones to not just make friends, but to make lifelong best friends, because of the internet — the kind of people for whom you'd cross an ocean and fall in love. My partner and I met on IRC, and our friendship developed and changed over the course of a decade, but we weren't the only ones. So many people came together, wanting to weave a network of shared knowledge and understanding, working to support the ones coming up after them. Some of us were lucky to have had teachers within these different communities, people who taught us how to use and think about the tools at our disposal. The list of people I owe is too long to even start, and grows so fast it'll never end, but the people in the IRC rooms, in LJ posts and comment threads and communities, in forums they created or even just helped maintain, they made me who I am, helped me start thinking about how I wanted to put this back into the world. They helped me think through my undergraduate degree, and they were there to support me while I fought to make sure my master's thesis on the role of magic in philosophy and religious studies was both taken seriously and understood.

As more and more people met on MMMORPGs or MUDDs or AIM or LJ, being taken seriously could become a challenge. For a long, long time we were told by people who didn't know what being in the ritual space of the 3 a.m. internet was like that our relationships were hollow or somehow less than "real life." But while these people saw these as dichotomies of life — Online and IRL — some of us knew the truth.

We knew that online life was always both real and unreal, that it was the distilled and crafted essence of self, but also the rawest, least curated version of who we really are, and that both of these things were true *because of* the other. And the ones who navigated that tension, who were *willing* to be buffeted and torn by it — to live in and work with it, to know ourselves and each other — were the ones who held and sustained a kind of arcane knowledge of how to move the world. We were the people who, in those weird and still spaces of vulnerability and longing, found the threads of connection and meaning that allowed many of us to shape art which showed others the truth of themselves.

My friends and I read new books about futuristic journalism, internet AI taking on the personages of Vodun Loa, pantheons of old and new gods roaming modern America, and the online world as a place where language and meaning could change reality. We crystalised our understandings of language as technology as magic; of gods of communication as personifications or hyper-compressed concentrations of certain conceptual perspectives; of every bit of the weird we knew as being made of will and perceptions and beliefs which could unfold out into the world, in just the right conjunction of time and place and people and need. We designed magazines that shaped culture, maintained collectives which everted the stories we'd been ingesting out into the world. We didn't just read about the architects of the future, we became them.

These powerful truths about how to cultivate connection and effect change were hidden, but they were available to be found by anyone; all we had to do was be willing to give ourselves over to being overwhelmed, be willing to be taken in and lose track of time in the rush of connecting to and creating a shared meaning with each other. All of which paradoxically meant the quiet process of sitting at a keyboard at 3 a.m. and reaching out into the darkness for a digital hand to hold. But this is power we're talking about, and just like any other powerful knowledge, there were some folx who took it and turned it inside out.

Since long before the internet there've always been people who only want power over others and did whatever they could to get it; online life just let them extend their reach. These folx were clever, smart, and skillful at causing rifts, or finding spaces in which they could leverage abuse. Folx whose only need was to cause trouble and turmoil in the communities that might otherwise have welcomed them in, who only wanted more drama, for its own sake. There were those cults of personality, stoked and maintained around the lure and pull of a name or a persona, that were, more simply, trolls working to prise apart the secrets of those around them, simply for the opportunity to do harm. Because the thing about offering yourself up on the altar of your community, about being open and vulnerable in that very public way, is that there is always the possibility that some people in the circle don't want to be a part of the communal ritual — they only want to know where to stick the knife, and to twist.

Sometimes I wonder if we might not all have been better off if more of us had shared the stories of our communities, earlier on — if we'd lived that experience louder and realised that there was a way to have the close, fervent intimacy of the comment thread, while still being able to take its meaning out to the world. Would we still have the same host of griefers, trolls, and marketeering magicians we have today? I wonder where we'd be if we'd been more insistent about telling our stories and having them understood, and if we'd all been familiar with the lessons of the Tungus shaman or the Native American medicine people.

Medicine people are there to help us navigate the nuances among and between this world and others, and to help us know what we need to do so that we can keep our selves and our communities' spirits in proper working order. For many cultures, medicine and spirit travel ceremonies were always community rituals, performed for the purpose of guiding members of the whole society and imparting knowledge that couldn't be gained any other way. But when white Western anthropologists found the psychedelic substances and practices of North American, South American, and African medicine and ceremonial people, they almost always abstracted those tools and practices, pulled them out of context and out of community, and somehow expected them to mean the exact same thing they did before. And, in a way, this is exactly what happened to those long-ago days of the internet.

The cultural leaders of the early-mid-2000s internet were operating at a moment when Western culture was seriously thinking about what "internet community" could really mean. Blogs and message boards and specific comment threads on particular nights of the week, all places created and maintained and facilitated by these gods of culture who'd crafted our references and our shared experiences, spaces where we might feel close to them, and because of them and the shared ritual spaces they curated, closer to ourselves. Night music radio transmissions of the romantically weird, doors held open for us to meet and show and offer up pieces of ourselves, to collaborate and know each other.

These people were — or should have been — the caretakers of something special; guides who travelled between multiple worlds, doing the crucial work of keeping safe all the others who travelled with them. But, at the same time, that early sense of camaraderie and mutual exploration led so many of us to think that a million flowers could truly blossom, all on their own. I wonder if we maybe didn't take enough care to safeguard and pass along the knowledge of how to cultivate the whole garden.

My understanding of magic and my life on the internet fed each other, grew each other, helped me define and engage with my self in relation to the other, because they were always bound up with that one same thing: intimacy. Specifically, that liminal, borderland sense of intimacy of whispered words and half-seen selves, in the dark. Everything I knew about magic came from that space, and everything about that space came with me onto the internet, and everything that era of the internet was helped me find the community I needed, where we could grow and shape that space, together. And in my heart and mind, and in everything I do online, I'm always trying to get back to that place, rebuild that type of community, re-experience that way of life: where it's always 3 a.m.

William Gibson described cyberspace as this other world made of binary code and otherworldly light; of collective unconsciousness and mutual hallucinatory states, somehow simultaneously hard-edged logic and swirling emotional matrix. But while this vision of the internet shaped so much of the 80s and 90s, what we made with each other in the early 2000s and 2010s defined our conception and expectations about what it meant to be online, and to be, online. A hearth-fire or a public house; a giant dinner party or a salon; and always at that moment where we all felt, together, like we were the last ones awake, talking long past 3 a.m., giving each other something crucial and meaningful that we would always be trying to replicate in the brighter light of the day.

IN THE FLESH

Sisonke Msimang

Manju calls on the hotel telephone line. I don't know how she knows where to find me but she does. It is late — close to midnight. I am at a conference, and when the phone rings I am in the shower, drunk and trying to sober up. It takes me a while to register that I should get out and pick up, but the phone keeps ringing and so I splash out messily and half-collapse on the bed naked. I almost laugh at myself. Alcohol makes me like this — smiley and silly until the moment I throw up. I take the phone off the cradle and it is Manju and she is crying and I am confused, not just because I am drunk but also because I am genuinely surprised that Manju has found me at all.

Manju with her dazzling smile and her long loose hair and her crazy Ghanaian-Indian accent — Manju who introduced me to the wonders of the online world. Manju who lives between Joburg and Accra and Geneva, who — like me — belongs more to the world than to one particular place. She is tender-hearted and I think maybe this is why she is crying now on the other end

41

of the line. But she doesn't give me time to finish the thought because she is answering a question my foggy brain hasn't allowed me to ask yet.

"It's Omololu," she says. "Hun, he's dead. He was shot. He was leaving the office and they killed him. It was instant."

There is more, but her words are a jumble of nonsense that ought to shame Africa and make the gods weep and still, today, they make no sense. Who were "they"? Why did they kill him? I do not understand what she is saying. We were online together yesterday. I teased him about his ceaseless work ethic. "Go home, you need to rest." I said this so many times and each time he would write back — quickly and with pointed humour — "And you?" He was always working, always pushing, never seeming to find it exhausting.

"They" were robbers. A group of armed men who attacked him minutes after he left a youth entrepreneurship meeting. They had no idea who he was or what his life meant to so many of us — those who had met him IRL and those who hadn't yet but who felt as though they had. So "they" tried to rob him and failed, and in the process, they robbed us all.

Omololu and I managed a listserv together which connected people working to address the AIDS crisis that was swallowing so many of our generation whole. He was a Nigerian activist and I was a South African one and somehow from the beginning, we understood each other. We worked across a large platform moderating the comments of hothead activists, coordinating approaches to major policy events. Pushing for an Africa that we imagined was possible — one where there was no AIDS. Or even better, an Africa where you could fuck as much as you liked without risking your life. Omololu would never have put it that way, of course. He was strait-laced and discreet — I wasn't, but that never seemed to get in the way of our friendship because he was so deeply committed to all the right things. Condoms were the right things. AIDS drugs for Africans were the right things. Justice was the right thing.

After a year or so, we transitioned into co-managing an advocacy campaign.

The internet was not so young then, but we were Africans and so it felt new to us — this virtual space we might use without having to make arduous flights that would force us to change planes in Europe only to return again to African destinations. We wanted to reshape the world and we had the audacity to think that we might make our own continent safer and healthier and better. We actually thought it was our right, believed vehemently that it was up to us to solve Africa's problems. We looked upon the do-gooder interns and the well-fed professors from North America with disdain. They were in our countries for a season while we were here for eternity.

Our parents had educated us to believe we could achieve anything. Omololu and I grew up in the 1970s when Africa was not a mess — it was a dream still being dreamed, promises kissed on the lips of children. Nigerians and Kenyans and Senegalese — we were proud and self-confident and our currencies were rising in strength and our cocoa beans and rice and plantains were worth so much on the open market. We did not yet understand that soon it would all be over, that overthrows by tinpot dictators propped up by the West would signal our demise, that our crops would soon be worthless, that our economies would become worthless. We did not know that famine would mark our continent and that we — the children who had been so proud — would beg to leave with suitcases full of pride and books and little else. Those of us who were lucky did leave. The rest stayed — praying for improvement, hoping for more than we had been given.

Then, in the 1990s, once we had come of age and challenged the strongmen, we began to reclaim our continent. We forced democracy down the throats of our fathers and we marched in the streets in country after country until ballot papers delivered us what we thought we needed. We insisted that Africa was ours to rebuild and soon there were Omololus everywhere, young Africans with the swagger of those who have nothing to lose and everything to gain. We were not starry-eyed and in this way we were different from our parents. We were tough and bold but soon enough even we — with our wary eyes and our guarded optimism — began to hope.

Then the internet came along and it made our pan-Africanism more than just a theory. Kenya's first president, Jomo Kenyatta, had once said, "Our children may learn about the heroes of the past. Our task is to make ourselves the architects of the future." Our generation — Omololu and myself and our entire cohort — thought the internet could deliver us this victory. We believed it could speed up the possible, that it could indeed help us to be the architects of our own futures.

Perhaps the mistake we made — because of those listservs and our activism in the real world — was that we overestimated our capacity to reimagine and reshape the world. The internet gave us unrealistic confidence. In this regard we were like humans everywhere. Our ability to conquer space and time merely with the press of a button, with the click-clack of our fingertips, made us omnipotent in our own minds.

We thought we were a new breed of African that would not yield to the tragic hand history had dealt us. We existed to defy the colonisers' predictions and to laugh in the faces of the gods of poverty and hopelessness that had thus far spared us no indignity. That we could organise a press release to denounce human rights violations in Congo even as we sat in Lagos and Johannesburg and Nairobi made us feel invincible. Armed with our hearts and our principles and the university degrees we had conjured with our grit and determination, we were unstoppable.

Omololu was the incarnation of all that activists like me stood for. He had been a journalist in a conventional newsroom, working for *PUNCH* magazine as a features editor. Then, as the AIDS crisis heightened, he had begun to see the importance of using his journalism skills to share knowledge with health professionals across the country. Omololu founded Journalists Against AIDS and soon, his work was borderless.

This was an age of innocence, before the idea of an armchair warrior would have made any sense. I worked for an organisation in Southern Africa that was interested in the same issues Omololu championed and so we teamed up. Soon we were working on an advocacy project in which we targeted African governments, challenging them to decriminalise sex work and homosexuality. We were ahead of our time, but we did not know it.

After working together online for months, we finally met. Omololu was dark and short and compact and so mild-mannered that at first I was taken aback. Was this the same man I had traded jokes with and organised alongside online? It was apparent very quickly that he was. He demonstrated the same level-headedness I had seen time and again on the list. He was principled and able to strategically decide what advocacy actions were necessary — when we should shout and when it would be better to whisper. There was a calmness to Omololu. He exuded this powerful sense that nothing was too big or hard for us to take on.

We established the African Civil Society Coalition on HIV and AIDS together. We used all our powers of persuasion to get African ministers to see that we didn't pose a threat — that we wanted to help them help our people. It worked, in large part because Omololu spoke so softly and yet so forcefully. He commanded respect without demanding it.

We had scored a big win — a declaration on health and rights in Africa that set new standards. We were riding high on that success and planning for more when the real world intruded as it so often does, and all of a sudden Omololu was gone. He was shot in the chest in a random act of violence. He lay dead in a pool of blood on a road in Lagos, surrounded by people and yet so alone because he could not be saved. And so much of me still today rejects the idea that it was random. I have no faith and so I cannot ascribe to it a higher meaning. Still, I want to believe it wasn't random. Even now, so many years later, I think if he had been a deliberate target on the basis of his work, then there might have been a target for our outrage, a place to throw our fury and our grief. It might have made more sense.

Instead Omololu was a victim of an ordinary crime. His killers were young men Nigeria had abandoned. They were like so many others who robbed and killed in order to eat, in order to feed their own families.

This is what we had not accounted for. We had — in our earnestness — lost sight of the externalities, which in Africa are always larger than life. We knew progress would not be a straight path and we understood that homophobia and sexism were our enemies, that poverty would confound our gains and stymy many of our efforts. This was part of the work. What we forgot was that at any moment, any of us in our coalitions and our task teams, with our internet connections and our fancy passwords, could be cut down by malaria or crime. We forgot that a car could crash on the dangerous roads that criss-crossed our continent. We forgot that our brains and our hearts and our dreams could not protect us from the vagaries of our continent, from the brutality of its history which snaked its way into our everyday in ways that could never be predicted.

Omololu's death diminished all of us. It made us believe less in ourselves and in the inevitability of our victory. Before he died, I never questioned that we would achieve our goals, and I never wondered if my generation would prevail in correcting the sins of our fathers.

After Omololu was killed, I doubted everything. I suddenly found it silly that a small group of young people believed they could turn the tide against a virus that was smarter and wilier than we could imagine. I suddenly realised the absurdity and arrogance of our quest. But it wasn't just our cause that felt fragile. Sitting on that bed half-drunk and naked, knowing that Omololu was gone forever, nothing felt as certain or clear. Our dreams were fragile and our bodies vulnerable, and yes — we were stoppable.

We continued to fight and we won many more battles. Today, the epidemic has subsided and many of the laws we fought against have been repealed. Still I have not recovered and never will. It was the work that tied us together, and also it was the internet. We met in the realm of the possible. We only came to know each other because we thought we were special. We became comrades because we were bold enough to believe our ideas deserved to zip through the air and arrive intact at their destinations.

When my friend died, I wanted to stop trusting the internet. It had given him to me through my screen and then he had been taken away from me in real life. Because of this — because this way of knowing someone was so new — I wanted to deny how much he had meant to me. It took me a long time to accept that I had loved him at all. I could not accept that he had been my co-conspirator, that I had come to rely on his steady presence which was as real as though he had been standing next to me when in fact he was on the other side of a continent. We only met a handful of times in real life, but I mourned him as I would have a brother. Until I met Omololu, I had no idea that you could trust someone you had never met, that you could love them so readily once you met them in the flesh. Omololu taught me many things, not least of all that on the internet — as in real life — there is no escaping love.

SOMMY

Ryan North

In 1996, feeling they were out of options, a family in the small town of Emeryville, Ontario, Canada, went to the media. They revealed that for months they'd been terrorised by a computer hacker who called himself "Sommy." He'd turn their TV and lights on and off. He'd eavesdrop on their private conversations and interrupt their phone calls first to burp at them, then to harass and taunt them in a disguised voice. The family — Dwayne and Debbie Tamai and their teenaged son, Billy — said they couldn't figure out what they'd done to earn Sommy's ire. All they knew was that the police were powerless to stop him, because unlike all the other criminals they'd encountered before, Sommy was committing his crimes over the internet. Sommy was committing a cyber crime.

It was a brief and unique era that seems impossible now: one in which more people had heard of computers and the internet than had actually used them. Adults without home or office computers — which is to say, most of them — got their

impressions of what the internet was like and what it was capable of from movies and actual cartoons. They said things like
"cyberspace" and "websurfing" and "information superhighway"
without a trace of irony. Hackers were seen as trickster gods:
wild but intelligent, capricious but untouchable — anger them
at your peril. A friend's father spoke often about hackers who'd
"trick you into downloading the entire Encyclopedia Britannica,
and then make your computer display it all at once, causing
your monitor to catch on fire." He believed this story no matter
what his son told him. He'd said he'd heard it on the news.

My friends and I — teenagers — knew this "Sommy" story was
complete baloney. We knew that computers and the internet
weren't and aren't magic, because we spent all our free time on
them. We knew that you couldn't take over someone's phone
line or light switches just by "hacking" them really hard, no
matter how talented you were. (That little trick would have to
wait a decade or two until we'd all invested in insecure internet-connected "smart devices.") A few days later the police had
a break in the case when they finally discovered that "Sommy"
was the family's teenage son, Billy, because of course he was.
Billy hadn't hacked anything — he just flipped three-way light
switches from the other room to mess with his parents, and
picked up the extra handset on their landline to tell them off in
a funny voice whenever he was mad at them. We knew this was
obviously the case the second the story broke, because the hacker
story was impossible. The only thing we didn't understand
was how the media, and the police, and Bell Canada — who'd
actually rewired the house several times trying to find how the
hacker was getting in! — could've been so stupid. In retrospect,
of course, the answer was obvious: the media and police and

even the telco companies weren't stupid, they simply were just not as extremely online as we were. They didn't know what they were talking about. But they'd get there.

We'd all get there eventually.

//

In February 2003, I started a webcomic, called "Dinosaur Comics," that I still update today: it's been the foundation of my entire career. It was one of the first online comics, and when it became popular, so did I. And this fame — this popularity with strangers who decided they liked my work and by extension me — literally changed me into a better person. I'd grown up shy; internet fame gave me self-assurance. I'd grown up insecure; internet fame made me confident. I'd grown up feeling that there was no one else like me in the world, and internet fame told me there were others out there and that they would love me and think I'm hilarious. It turns out that the anonymous love of strangers — even if you'll never meet most of them — is enough to turn you into a better person, more friendly, confident, relaxed in your own skin. I know it, because it made me who I am today.

It did all that because early-internet fame had three properties that made it great: it was opt-in, it was pseudo-anonymous, and it was incredibly fun. The web still had that allure of being somewhat underground — not everyone was on it and we all knew someone who was just getting their first email address — which made it separate and distinct from the real world. Because of that, any internet fame was automatically self-limiting: if I ever did get a big head from people loving me online, that would be counteracted by me going outside and nobody knowing who I am. Even if the media somehow reported on you — astronomically unlikely — it'd be in the same tone they'd use when they went down to the county fair to cover some record-breaking giant zucchini or a prize-winning cow: amusement, mixed with a hint of condescension, so that everyone knew they were all just playing along with the joke. It was as if they were saying good for you, zucchini and cow. But come on, we're all just having a bit of fun and big zucchinis, special cows, and people with websites don't REALLY count. This isn't real life, and you're not THAT famous.

We don't make fame like that anymore.

//

I have a nephew, Davis, who is young, but old enough now to read and write and easily savvy enough to know that if everyone around him is looking at screens, then he wants a screen to look at too. He's in the first generation to be raised with ubiquitous internet wherever he goes, one you can't quit, one that does count. His internet is way more powerful than mine ever was when I was coming up: his has video to better livestream and glorify mass killings, shadowy misinformation campaigns to better nudge his beliefs towards something more useful (or profitable) to anyone willing to pay, and social media to better ruin his life should he ever tweet something thoughtless and stupid before getting on a plane for eleven hours.

In middle school he will have classmates who already have internet fame and who post videos of themselves almost daily — got to keep the algorithm happy — and he might feel jealous of that and try to think of ways that he can get more strangers to like him online too. In high school his popularity

will be precisely and publicly quantified not just by his follower and like and subscription counts, but by the corporations
providing him those numbers. All my embarrassing juvenalia
is lost forever — there was no money to be made in storing it
back then — while it's likely that everything he ever posts will
be archived and analysed by countless parties with countless
motives, to be examined algorithmically when he wants insur-
ance, when he wants a job, when he wants a new hot water
heater. And despite all of this, it may still be an entirely reasonable thing for him to pursue some measure of internet fame
as soon as possible, just as soon as he can, because then if he
ever gets cancer or leukemia or chronic obstructive pulmonary
disease or any of the countless other diseases that can strike him
randomly and unfairly at any point in his life, his GoFundMe
will have a much greater chance of succeeding.

Please RT.

//

In 2003, only a week after I'd started Dinosaur Comics, I met
my best friends, Joey and Emily. Joey emailed me to say he'd
read my comics and to ask me what I'd do with my Nobel
Prize for Comics money, and he sent me a link to the comic
he and Emily had just started, called "A Softer World." We
didn't know we were all best friends forever then, obviously,
but we did soon enough. I sent Emily letters through the mail
because she had a typewriter and I had a typewriter and we
both wanted to use them, but Joey and I emailed. It didn't take
long before they were incredibly honest letters, sent in plain
text on an unencrypted connection, because nobody cared
but us. We went through breakups at the same time and we

helped each other through them and I'd never connected with someone like that before. He got pure honesty from me, and I got pure honesty from him. I've never gone back to re-read those emails because even now they're too real, and because I'm worried that I won't respond to them in the same way now as I did then, and that would lessen them somehow, and I don't ever want them lessened. They belong to us, the Ryan and Joey of 2003 and 2004.

When I moved to Toronto in 2005 and didn't know anyone, Joey got two of his Toronto friends, Tim and Ro, to invite me — a complete stranger — over for dinner and board games. I was so excited and so eager and young and naive that I showed up at 5 p.m. for an 8 p.m. dinner invitation, because I didn't want to be late. Tim and Ro were gracious enough to invite me in and help them clean and cook, and that ongoing and lasting friendship with those two became the seed from which all my relationships in Toronto — where I still live — came from. They gave me a community, a friend group, and a social life where before I had none. I married Jenn after going to a book launch with Kean, who I met at a comics event with Ro, who I know through Joey and Emily, who I met through comics, which I started because I loved the internet and wanted to spend all my time there. My friends, my wife, my personality, my career — I'd have none of them without the internet giving me a home in 2003, changing the course of who I was and what I'd become. The internet has been, without exaggeration, the single greatest positive force in my life, something objectively and intrinsically good for me.

And yet.

//

And yet, I'm not sure how to reconcile the internet Davis will face — exploitative, inescapable, dangerous — with the internet I had when I was in my early twenties and alone in the biggest city in Canada. We were all techno-utopians then: the internet would connect everyone on the planet with everyone else in a forum where we could all be whoever and whatever we wanted, and nobody could do a thing to stop us. Everything was up for discussion, and ideas would survive or fail based solely on their merit. In a space where everyone could talk to everyone and nobody knew you were a dog, the marketplace of ideas would save us, because it was a crucible that would produce only pure, freebased truth. And if we didn't quite have it yet, we'd have it soon. This was what we were leaving to those who came after us, and for a while, it did feel like that was what we had. But it couldn't last, it would never last, because we'd made the same mistake that everyone makes when planning utopia: we were humans, and we thought we were better than we were.

We didn't know that letting everyone talk to everyone else anonymously simply meant anyone who stood out could be harassed by a faceless, unstoppable, literally endless mob of hate, even while they slept. We somehow missed that if anything was up for discussion and you were marginalised in any way, then you'd be required to debate your basic right to exist, over and over, with someone whose only goal is to see you fail. We never foresaw that if your mistakes were always available online — which they would be, because screenshots are free and the whole purpose of computers is to organise and store and share data — then you could never be allowed to move past them, because there would always be someone who just today posted something you said or did without the context of your growth and education and regret and apologies since then, so that someone else could see for the first time the person you used to be but no longer are and be outraged anew.

We let people say the internet "didn't count" because we knew it did, and then woke up one day to discover that we were right all along and now it counted more than anything else. Now it would change the course of lives, elections, countries, civilisations, and it would do that even if you never logged in once in your life because it changed everything and everyone, no take-backsies.

//

The basic structure of this essay has been "good internet thing, bad internet thing, good internet thing, bad internet thing." It's built that way because I'm struggling with two fundamentally irreconcilable facts. The first fact is that that the internet has inarguably been a good force in my life, giving me a personality, a life, a career. I spent all my time online then, and I spend all my time online now.

The second fact is that I'm horrified at the thought of my nephew doing the same.

Is there a place he can go that's hidden from the outrage mobs and doxxing and swatting and endless digging through post histories to find receipts? A place where a weird kid can be a weird kid and find his tribe as he figures himself out, without worrying that in fifty years when he's running for office someone will try to dig up what he posted and use it to destroy him? And if that place exists, will it be populated by people who have either forgotten or never knew how to weaponise anonymity and the police, who have never seen someone use their own

followers as an outrage mob sent against their chosen target?
And if there is a place, and he finds it, can he learn enough
in time to avoid what he posts being tracked by his ISP and
advertisers and Facebook and research agencies and foreign
powers and his own government?

Sommy can't happen anymore. We are all online and too
many of us know what the internet can and cannot do. But in
that brief and unique era that seems impossible now, when
Sommy COULD happen, you could do other things too. You
could make friends for life on a platform that didn't carry a risk
of ruining your life. You could have overwhelmingly positive
experiences online for days, weeks, years at a time.

And some kid and his friends could know more about computers than any of the adults in the room.

I wish Davis the confidence and joyful experience that comes
with that, to never encounter people or platforms that want to
destroy him, and to at least once touch the wonder of imagining what the world will be like in ten, twenty, fifty years now
that it has him — and this wonderful new technology of the
internet — in it.

And I wish him luck.

TO ESCAPE, YOU MUST'VE BEEN BRAVE

Anaïs Escobar Mathers

I used to be the girl who brought you her heart not
on a sleeve but on a platter, messed up and confused
and confusing; good for reading, bad for living.

I was twenty-two and lost when I chose youveescaped as a
Tumblr username on a whim, the title of a song from a band
I no longer listen to. It sounded evocative and seemed like the
invitation I wanted to extend to myself at that point to go somewhere new. I had no idea what I was doing. I had transferred
to a new college after having had a bit of a breakdown at the
first one and was flailing as an attempt at living. It's strange to
think that this was the beginning of almost everything else that
has happened since.

I had taken time off from school and so I was still in the
middle of my BA at twenty-two. I had moved closer to home

due to the breakdown as well as the fact that my beloved aunt, more like my older sister really, was slowly dying of kidney disease. I was in a relationship with a man who lived a thousand miles away and had found a way to simultaneously control me and not really give a shit about me. I was a ghost of a girl, going through the motions and not really fully present anywhere. Now I know that I was suffering from PTSD caused by an abusive childhood, but back then, in that moment, I just felt out of step with everything. I was that most dangerous combination of so sad but still hopeful. But I couldn't talk to anyone in my real life — the wall I'd built was too tall. I was so lonely but had no idea how to open up to people.

On Tumblr I wrote with a sort of freedom that felt unlike anything I had ever experienced before. For months I talked to whoever was on the other side of a blinking cursor, not being careful like I was in writing workshops. I wrote about my past romantic relationships, my family, my childhood — myself really, for the first time ever. It was just me and these words and it felt good if not a little self-indulgent. I told myself I would shut it down or make it private, make sure it didn't get out into the world before I applied for grad school or jobs; I didn't, though. I was so afraid to open myself up that I have no clear memory of actually deciding to, but I tagged my posts with the writing tag, guaranteeing people would see it. I couldn't have said this to myself then, but even though it scared me, I wanted this.

Back then the only "engagement" Tumblr had was likes or reblogs; the more I wrote, the more the likes began to roll in, but the reblogs were what really got my attention. People reblogging my writing and saying "This is good" or "Me too!" or "I've experienced this" made me feel seen in a way I'd never been before. These people, my future best friend among them, were mostly strangers to me. It made me feel like maybe the things I had to say were important and relatable. At the very least, somebody felt they were worth reading. Somewhere between telling myself I would make it private and actually doing it, I got my first follower. And then another. And another. It made me nervous and excited all at once. I now had regular readers and I didn't want to disappoint. The more I was read, the more desire I had to share.

//

> You ran down to the dark water and found him wait-ing there. You noticed how much taller he was out of the water, how tall he was for fifteen. You sat on the sand together, tucking your feet underneath you. You learned about each other and that you had nothing in common but you closed your eyes when he leaned in to kiss you. You kissed in the dark, his hands on your still hipless body, yours on his warm shoulders. You wondered if his hands could keep you from floating off the sand. You worried he'd realize you only had mosquito bites. You only opened your eyes when you felt eyes on you. You saw your dad standing on the porch from yards away and knew he knew that you knew that he knew what you were doing. You squeezed his hand and ran back to the house past your dad and directly to bed.

I typed with abandon and a sense of anticipation, hungry for the responses, clicking "post" always with a tingle of nerves but mostly ready for the sensation of putting myself out there, of hearing back. I talked about the time I got drunk at junior prom and dived into the shallow end of a swimming pool, smashing up my face. I talked about my grandparents emigrating from Cuba to the US and their struggles to build a new life for themselves in a country where they didn't even speak the language. I talked about the house I grew up in and how it may be haunted. I wrote a series called the Love Notebooks which explicitly got into the realities of my past romantic relationships. I talked about the end of the romantic relationship I was in as well as the ones that followed. I talked about my difficult relationship with my mom. I talked about my aunt only in her thirties when she passed away and what it was to go through grief for the first time in my life. I talked about my life through looking back at memories and also in real time — the grief of loss, of heartbreak, fresh on the page for whoever came across it. It felt electric.

It was exhilarating to write and share on Tumblr because I was finally able to be open about the things that had happened to me. To delve into a relationship post-mortem was freeing and powerful; to put the details of what had happened both in good times and bad made me feel strong. These stories were raw, especially when it came to sexuality, and I didn't spare any details. How someone's skin felt against mine, the scent of a partner, the feeling of someone's fingers pressed against me — all of these things were out there and a part of my stories. They were specific and didn't pull any punches. The feedback was effusive and I relished hearing from readers who could relate to the heartache and the relationships I wrote about. I wouldn't have believed it when I first started but I felt proud of what I was writing.

Of course, I still sometimes worried I was oversharing, but I couldn't deny how real and good it felt to be vulnerable, to connect with others. I was writing about how I lost my virginity in graphic detail or how I had cheated on a past partner, and all I could feel was a relief at being able to put it into words, to be able to turn so many moments that were awkward or painful into something more beautiful than what had actually happened. The posting became something I needed, a way to process first by myself through writing, but then also through others' consumption of my thoughts made public, their voices talking back to me. I was writing about things I could hardly bring up with my IRL friends but which felt different and safe in this place online. I truly found a home at this URL.

I didn't always like what readers had to say, but for the most part, I was able to find a safe space with other people, something I had never really experienced before. There are faces and names from that time that I still talk to now, that I'm still friends with. These relationships grew and remain strong to this day. Some of these friendships began to extend IRL and I connected with people on a deeper level. Some remained usernames and icons that I can still remember clearly as if I was looking at them for the first time. My readership grew into the tens of thousands, blowing up into something bigger than I could have imagined, and I still craved the response, the acknowledgement. I couldn't get enough of really putting myself out there, of finally being heard.

//

You don't forget though. I've made peace with what's happened, stopped trying to make sense of such a senseless thing as death. It's not death that haunts me but the memory, the living, the things that came before it all ended. It's the knowledge and absence of what I've lost that hurts the most; this is my ghost. It never stops hurting, the big losses never do; it becomes a part of your bones. It rips you apart and leaves you to figure out what to do next. This ghost has informed how I choose to live, what I do, how I love. You will ache and you will hurt but you will be feeling, remembering not just the pain but how much love there was and how much there still is; death can never touch that.

My life was online. I went to school, went to work, had IRL friends, but the real living was happening online. I was connecting with people who lived a world away and building relationships that I never expected to make. I lived publicly online and I became used to sharing everything. When I broke up with that man who lived a thousand miles away, I shared it on my blog, and the outpouring of support and love (with a smattering of judgement) got me through a truly terrible time. I also experienced the surreal nature of being a somewhat public person going through something like a breakup when I discovered readers talking about my relationship and breakup on their own blogs. "If youveescaped and her boyfriend can't make it work, how can I?" one post read; it shook me to realize that others thought of what was happening in my life as something to relate to like this. It was no mystery, since everything about my life was online, but it was still beyond surreal.

I delved into darker things like grief, a shattering from the inside out for me. I couldn't handle the grief of losing my aunt so suddenly and I put that into words as much as I could. I was walking around just broken inside and I couldn't figure out how to process things alone. Having the space to sound things out, to write my way out of my hole, saved me. I was so low and I was able to crawl back to solid ground through working through it in this space my readers and I made together over the years. It kept me sane, it kept me alive. My readers reached out with stories of losing family and loved ones and made me feel less alone. One reader sent me a beautiful hummingbird pendant with a thoughtful card and it was a lighthouse for me; I felt as much as I needed to, out loud, online — something I wasn't getting or, maybe, allowing myself to get IRL.

My little community grew into a bigger one and I recognised that it was becoming bigger than anything I had ever expected. Tumblr was a place where I put the most real parts of myself, the messy and the raw. I wrote about my mom's alcoholism before I told some people IRL. I wrote about being sexually assaulted at age seventeen before I told many people IRL. But what happens when the place you make for your secrets becomes well known? Well, things get weird. The feedback that you're hearing grows louder and you start getting trolls and naysayers. It becomes a shaky balance between the excitement of putting yourself out there and the nerves that come from anticipating what the response might be. Brains are so good at remembering every word of a hurtful comment, and I have a few of those still lodged in there from that time. There was a very specific comment about my sideburns that will always float around my brain waiting for moments when

I'm not feeling great about myself to show its face again. The more attention I got, the more of myself was on display to be criticised. It was a lesson in being vulnerable in public and realising that you have no control over what other people will think of you. It gave me a tougher skin; it taught me that I could survive differences of opinions and reactions I didn't like.

I think the special thing about this time is the feeling of intimacy between you and the people who read you, who you interacted with. It was a small world even when it really wasn't. It is sometimes astounding to me that it's been over a decade with many of these people, these friends, and we are still in each other's lives. I survived this time of my life because of community and the people who were there from the beginning with me, who grew to be friends and sometimes even family. I reconnected with my now-best friend through Tumblr, years after having been high school acquaintances, and they were able to see all sides of the person I was becoming, connecting the person I was IRL with the openness of self on my blog. Our relationship showed me that I could be open in my actual life, that I didn't have to separate the parts of me I was nervous about. It was the first step.

//

I guess what I mean is that you can't make something, money or art or anything, for the sake of making it; it's missing something in the process that way. It turns out there's time enough for everything if you don't force it, and that goes for the right person, too.

How do you merge all the versions of yourself into who you want to be? For a while, it did feel like a divide existed: being so authentic and open online while keeping a wall up IRL. I built that wall to keep me safe, in a place where I wouldn't have to confront things, only to find myself blossoming as my readers, and now my best friend, continued to reach past it. At some point, the feeling of being split between that growth and what I was walling myself off from seemed to fade away; it's almost as if the part of me growing and blossoming, this online part of me, just reached over my wall to all the other parts that were so scared to be myself and be open and made them realize it was okay. Not only was it okay to do the difficult thing I thought of as "being myself," but it was okay to just *be*.

I felt freer as a result of this growth, as if I didn't have anything to hide or be ashamed of. It changed how I functioned IRL and in relationships by showing me how to be vulnerable, that there is strength in letting others in and letting them see the parts of myself I was scared to show them. I never consciously intended to use a blog to let others in, but some part of me knew better and understood that I needed to break down that wall my upbringing and trauma had built. It made me more balanced as a person, helped me learn that there is nothing wrong with sharing what I'm feeling with the people in my life, that my feelings are valid. I discovered that there was room for me in my own life. Just like with my best friend who I had allowed to climb over my wall, I realized how to let other people in my life.

Eventually, I let my IRL friends begin to read my writing and learn things about me that I didn't know how to bring up face to face. Things about my childhood, my worst fears, my hopes for the future — all of it right there in prose for them to take in and really understand. There were some awkward conversations about why I didn't feel comfortable just talking about these things, but for the most part, people understood how special this was, how necessary it was not just for me to process things but to share them in this very specific space. The more time passed, the more it felt like the separate versions of myself, both online and IRL, started to become one. I became more myself the more I put myself out there. In a turn I never expected, I brought my online writing to my writing workshop and found that it did make sense there; I have never felt prouder to get positive feedback from my classmates than on the Love Notebooks. I had finally merged my online and IRL lives and was reaping the benefits.

Having a Tumblr brought me some of the best things in my life. It brought me to a place where I became a writer, it brought me opportunities to write for other places, it brought me friends. It even brought me my husband. He started out reading my writing and we followed each other's Tumblrs and began talking from there. He was in Canada and I was in Florida and I asked myself, "Why are you talking to this guy in Canada?" But our relationship began because of Tumblr, the witness at our elopement was a friend of mine from Tumblr, and I mean, I live in a different country now because of this blog I decided to randomly start one day. My life is exactly where it is today because of the internet, because of the people who talked back to me and taught me it was okay to connect with others. Life is so strange and beautiful.

//

I felt myself sacrificing the possibility of a life at different points to pursue something I wasn't even sure
why I was doing. I filled my life and head with noise
to the point where I couldn't be alone with myself;
this part of me, when in check, is wonderful and valu-
able but it's easy to get lost in facts, in other people's
stories instead of writing your own.

I shut down the blog a few years ago because I reached a
point where I had said what I needed to say on it; it served its
purpose and its time. It's weird shutting the door on something
so important to you, but I got all the best that I could from that
little Tumblr: love, family, friends, self. The internet was more
intimate in those days, still big, but it felt smaller. We weren't
overwhelmed by social media options yet; we had just a few
places to build communities. It felt so special and lucky. I have
a newsletter these days because I haven't lost that urge to sometimes connect with those people still reading, and it's amazing
to me that there are still people reading and speaking back to
me. It's an honour really. Like on Tumblr, I use the newsletter
to process the things going on in my life. I talk about my mom
passing away of cancer. I talk about the chronic illness I've
been diagnosed with. I talk about deciding whether or not to
have a kid. I talk about my life, which despite everything the
world throws at it, is a good one.

They say that everything you do leads you to the moment
you're at, and it's still astounding to me that the decision to
start a Tumblr was one of those little things that was actually
a hugely important moment. I took my broken heart and put it
into words so many times and it saved me. In hindsight, I know

I was looking for something even if I didn't know then what it was. I was looking for a voice, looking to be whole, looking to be heard. And I got so much more than that.

OUR SECOND LIFE

James Mitchell

One Saturday morning, my brother and I were watching TV when Mum came downstairs and said, "Boys, I've met a man." Jack was nine at the time, but at seventeen, I considered myself Mum's agent, and as agent, I thoroughly approved, and said so. And Mum might have considered me her agent too, because she next had to check we were happy with the details.

"He's a man on the internet."

Today, there are many men on the internet. (The internet thrums, surges with men, to the point where good people often decide there are, if anything, too many, and take a break.) But it was 2002, and the idea of meeting a man on the internet was about as plausible as, say, buying a book on the internet.

You'd find it even stranger if you knew our mum, sixteen years ago. The way she told us, sidling in to request that she be able to look for love in a manner that wouldn't disrupt our cartoons, carried the reserve she had when it came to men. Her relationship with Dad hadn't been a happy one, in a way that I never fully understood because — and I'm only grasping this now — she hid it so well, two closed doors away from wherever I was in the house. If he ever did Dad stuff, like picking me up from school or putting a pizza in the oven, I thought he was unbelievably cool doing it. Perhaps because he was so funny. Perhaps because whatever he was doing, it seemed like he had better things to do. Perhaps this is why he was only my dad about fifty percent of the time.

After he left to become my dad zero percent of the time, Mum made some attempts to meet people, but what do you do when you're a primary school teacher in a small town in South East England? Mrs Claire Mitchell was every child's favourite, and she was always invited to the gatherings of well-meaning parents, but she felt keenly the sense of other people's charity, and she winced every time she was summoned to yet another friend's granite kitchen island to meet "someone we think you'll really like." The daytime? Most of her colleagues were children. And she didn't want to stand around at the bar of the Slug and Lettuce, waiting for divorcées to talk to her ("Didn't you teach my Faye?"). Or, if she did want to hit the town, she buried it deep because she had two needy boys to look after. When it comes to love, honest physical serendipity is the dream, but when you spend years walking the world without meeting anyone remotely like you and single, well. You could meet anyone online. A millionaire stepfather, imagine that. In that moment in front of the TV, I did.

Dave — davebyus, if we're talking usernames — was a locksmith in Visalia, California. That's California, America, the America of films and rich friends' holidays. Friends with two parents. Dave had experienced his own marriage falling apart, had his own children, and like Mum, hadn't come to the internet asking for love. Even if OKCupid had existed at the time, I think they'd both given up on love, or assumed they'd had their fair share of it in their lives already. They found each other without looking. "You know I'm doing this writing course online," Mum said to us. I'd read her short stories, written in round teacherly handwriting on A4 lined paper. "He's doing it too." Some pre-algorithmic twist of fate had put them in the same study group of a Writers' Village University course, and there they'd started discussing each others' work, and then each other, Mum taking the house phone up to her room or out to the garden for an hour at a time. Yes, I'd noticed this, when I looked up from *Final Fantasy VIII* for long enough. After she worked up the courage to send him her address, he sent her letters and mixtapes like a true courting Californian: I remember a burned CD of Crosby, Stills, Nash & Young with a handwritten tracklist and doodles on the back. And now that I knew about him, I got mail, too. A handwritten letter with a dollar, the first I'd held, and a pocket-sized copy of the Constitution. The letter was short and funny, just one scribbled leaf torn from a reporter's notepad. Something about it being sunnier there. "Your mom tells me you're about to study politics." It ended with a dirty limerick. Alright, I thought, as I folded the dollar into my Animal surfer's wallet. You can stay.

Two months after the letter, Mum flew to California for one week, and Jack and I settled at our grandparents', in the room where Mum and her sister had slept as children. We spent a long day with the usual distractions, kicking the deflated ball against the garage wall and watching animated *Robin Hood*. In the evening, the telephone rang in the study. Grandma went upstairs to answer it, then called down for me. An endless climb later, I put the phone to my ear, and:

"He's wonderful. He's asked me to marry him, and I've said yes."

//

She came back happy. Happy, in a way I'd assumed parents could not be. Hungry for life, eager for time to move on to the next, brilliant thing. And the next thing would be brilliant, for Dave made plans to visit us in the summer. We drove to Heathrow Airport to pick him up, stood in front of the tiny door marked Arrivals, and waited for this man to emerge onto British soil. An hour went by. The people from his LAX flight passed us, hugged their families. Then Mum's flip-phone rang, and she scrambled in her bag for it.

Dave had been held at the border. A lone man who's not dressed for business and hasn't left his country in the fifty-some years of his life raises eyebrows at Heathrow. He shared such earnest excitement with Mum, I imagine he earnestly told an unsmiling border officer he was going to visit the family of his fiancée who he met on the internet; see, here's the baseball bat I've brought her children, I hope they like me. Mum was summoned to Immigration from the other side, and while we waited at the gate, they sat parallel interviews: yes, they'd met online. A writing website, yes. Yes, they were getting married — no, not yet, he has a ticket home, we're doing it all above board, we're good people. Another hour later, he was released — they were released, together, and walked out of Arrivals looking like they had always been together and free. He shook my hand like an equal, but after that I sat with Jack in the back of the car where I should have always been. Dave sat in the front with Mum, and suddenly, finally, our little car was full of family.

The fortnight passed like a film. The places we'd always been felt renewed: the garden, the kitchen, our little town — now truly inhabited by a complete us, with this happy scarecrow of a man gazing at everything, mouthing every -shire and -borough on the road signs. Jack and I took him to the park: a little field behind the house bordered by the trees, the church, and the town cricket club. It turned out I was terrible at baseball, he was terrible at football — our football — and Jack was brilliant at both. And just as that incredible life began to feel like something we deserved, Dave had to go home, to transform back from vital reality into a voice, a letter, a username. Something had changed for me, though. School was charged with a new energy. I represented a family, with a family's future, not just an individual life trying to sweep up the past into something whole. I told my best friend Alex about "Dave in America"; maybe I would go to college there. Half the school (the half that could get in) made a pilgrimage to see *American Pie 2*, and I thought that even the life of its most unfortunate character would make for a good future, if only I could get it.

//

The summer holidays: my memory of the Valley is all senses. Visalia was a four-hour straight-line drive from LAX through desert and vineyard, and Dave's old pickup did it both ways, his hand on her thigh the whole return journey, in a way that seemed to me like it must have always been there. Dry heat on the dust, the shocking blast of an air-conditioned Save Mart doorway, the radioactive mouthfeel of a huge slurpee. In the Sequoia National Forest, the sounds of a bear snuffling near our tent at night; the thump of a fist-sized pinecone on the forest floor in the morning. And one scene, remembered in full: a truck drive up winding mountain roads into that forest, listening to *Moon Safari* by Air and feeling like Dave was confidently driving us up out of the sad, small lives we had once led and into a new world.

Today we are all used to the idea of the internet granting us an alternative life. A new name, new values, friendships, status. But this felt like new life beyond a login. In this life, whenever I spoke, people turned to listen. People overheard me and gasped, "Harry Potter!" The most famous English boy in America. (You know, the boy who slept in a cupboard under the stairs, until a letter arrived and changed everything?) The first house party I went to was in the apartment above Dave's. A confident girl named Georgia pointed at the Homer Simpson poster on her wall and demanded: "Do you know who this is?" I crept back downstairs at 2 a.m. as the party drifted to a close. My head buzzing with cicadas and booze, I wondered what miracle had given me this body to wear, and if I'd ever have to give it back.

Girls actually talking to you. Parties where you belong. The measures of meaning in a heterosexual teen boy's life are so simple. But each of us was given what we needed: Jack, a real male role model who was there when he said he would be; Mum and Dave, someone to laugh with, make plans with, play CDs to. When we came home for the new school year, I could not say which life was the real one. Only one had a defined future. They'd get married, we'd apply for green cards, and all the while I would sit my A-levels and finish a British education, while trying to work out how I might pay for US college. An outlandish, half-formed plan, but stranger things had already happened.

In September, we returned for the wedding. Just Mum, Jack, and me. With family supportive but absent, it felt like an elopement. Mum and Dave couldn't afford a full service, and they didn't really want one. Instead, we made that same drive up the mountains, the four of us in a rented Dodge Ram, followed by our friends from Dave's apartment and his pastor, also called Dave. We couldn't reach the summit as planned because it had snowed and we didn't have tyre chains, so our convoy became a congregation halfway up at a mountain creek. Pastor Dave led us to a rocky outcrop, tiered geology cascading around and holding up the widest of skies above us. Mum and Dave stood before him, and we stood beside our mum, and witnessed only by five friends and a rushing river, the pastor asked a teacher and a locksmith who'd met on a forum if they would take each other as husband and wife.

They'd written their own vows. We have the magic and the mystery, Mum said. The high air whipped her words away as she spoke them and made her tresses dance. We'd never seen her like this. Jack smiled at me. We came down from a different mountain than the one we'd climbed.

//

The three of us returned to England to pack up our affairs, guide immigration papers through channels (Claire Byus, the well-practiced new signature read), and let me take my exams. Until our new life began, we had to pretend the old one was still valid. The internet and phone was where Mum and Dave (Dad? Not yet, but I knew it could happen) had their extended honeymoon. And of course, they kept writing fiction, sending each other stories. It makes me sad that at the time, I didn't really care that much, and I never asked Dave to read his writing. Years later, the website where they'd met bought and published one of Dave's stories, and as I began to write, I studied it. "A Wish For Jackie" was 1,708 words of perfectly formed, wide-eyed-but-wise fable. It was anchored by emotion, quietly meticulous, and unpretentious. A Californian locksmith of a story.

Dave had never met Mum's parents, and since they'd looked after Jack and me for that first-ever visit, he owed them a visit of his own. He came for Valentine's Day, 2004, a cold week: we played Scrabble in our little kitchen; lost him, for a heart-stopping half minute, in Central London; braved icy wet wind on the battlements of Windsor Castle. On the last day, he sat on the sofa with a box of tissues and a Lemsip. Surely it wouldn't hurt to stay a couple of days and rest? But there was nobody to run the shop. Keys always need cutting. We prepared to return to the old life, a marriage held together by Atlantic cable.

That's how Dave called Mum the next day, to say he'd gone to the Kaweah-Delta Medical Center, been diagnosed with "a bad cold, maybe asthma," and sent home with an inhaler to look after himself. He had a novel I'd lent him; he'd hole up in bed with that and let the sickness wash out of his lungs. He'd stay in touch. We went to school, and school, and work; we lived, and waited. That's what you do when you can't be there.

We got home, and the phone rang upstairs in Mum's room, as promised. Mom went to answer, then called for me. An endless climb later, I was sitting on the bed next to her. Mum hadn't put the phone on speaker but I could hear that it was Sarahelena, Dave's downstairs neighbour. We barely spoke to her, had no cause to.

"Are you sitting down?" she said.

So people really say that, went my dumb thought.

I went downstairs first. To get out of the bedroom where time wouldn't budge. So I saw Jack, standing at the bottom of the stairs below me, looking up in a question. Nobody had taught me how to say such a thing any more than they'd taught me how to hear it. It shouldn't be something that's just blurted out to you; you should already know, you should see it happening slowly, in a quiet room, you should have time to make peace with the idea that —

"Dave's dead."

My brother's face collapsed. That was the moment when I understood how much Jack really loved him. And how much I loved him, too. Behind us, halfway up the stairs, Mum sagged to the landing and let out a scream that filled our house. A single, violent noise from the centre of her.

In all the travel and tearing up visas and packing up lives that followed, all of the grief and the awkward pity and the silence that came to fill the empty seat in our lives to come, she would never repeat that noise where we could hear. She didn't have to, because its meaning was clear: the end of everything, for all of us, forever.

//

It seems incredible to me now, at thirty-three. Sitting at the kitchen table and sifting through the story while my loving

partner sleeps in — my impossibly special someone, in a bed
just a room away, and yet we communicate over the internet
more often than Mum did with her husband in another country.
Would they have sent each other emojis, GIFs? What would
our family WhatsApp group be like? Mum did not find another
partner — you can't follow that — but carried on as though nothing had happened. Or so it might seem, but there are clues of
the magic it worked within her. One big thing: she became a
foster parent, using the best of her teaching to show desperate
children a world as new to them as the Valley was to us. If
your heart can send you across the sea via a message board,
what can't it do?

But the small things are big things, too: the American flag
on the wall of Jack's room, and the dollar, framed, in mine,
like waking from a dream of the sea to find a shell in your
pocket. And the name Claire Byus, once signed, was never
undone. The laminated Comic Sans labels on classroom doors
carried the same name that fell from the lips of a thousand
grateful students: Mrs Byus. She gets stopped in our hometown by those children now, some as adults with children of
their own. She doesn't tell the story to any of them, of course,
and neither Jack nor I tell it much to anyone else, perhaps
because it sounds so sad that it feels like handing someone
a thing they don't know what to do with. Perhaps because it
seems so much like a story, and every year that passes now
can make it seem more so.

But for anyone who's been shown a future, then had the
door slammed shut in their face, know this: this life that is
happening now is not just the old one, grudgingly restarted. It
is something else, newly touched by darkness, light, and love.

The three of us met the man behind davebyus, a man with a calm smile and soft grey hair and open eyes, and now we walk the world with that openness. We are forever open to chance, to change, to a miracle, and this, this is our second life.

LIVING BETWEEN WORLDS

Mohale Mashigo

I was born in 1983, which technically makes me a millennial. According to headlines, I don't own a home and cannot afford diamonds because I eat too much avocado. I'm a millennial in many ways (hello, avocado; goodbye, ridiculous capitalism) but in some ways, I consider myself a Gen X leftover.

Being a black child born in apartheid South Africa and growing up in Nelson Mandela's "Rainbow Nation"[1] meant that many of my experiences mirrored those of Gen X. I was on the cusp of two generations in a way that would make me a perpetual late bloomer. Thanks, South Africa (insert side eye and a sigh). All the images that pop up when you think of late bloomers probably apply to me, so I won't bore you with details of high school crushes who wanted to "go all the way"

---

1 *A phrase coined by Nobel Laureate Archbishop Emeritus Desmond Tutu, describing post-apartheid South Africa.*

when I just wanted to make out. I was also late in getting online. I didn't grow up in a home with a PC. My father had one at work, but according to him, that is exactly where computers belonged: in an office building for people who had jobs.

But I am a nerd who obsesses over things I love. If I love it, then I have to know everything about it — and that's what started my life on the internet. Like most teenage girls, I had fallen victim to the boy band phenomenon. It was the late 90s; Thabo Mbeki was South Africa's second democratically elected president, and I was a huge fan of any kind of music sang by boys who had inexplicably bad dance moves. My favourite was a group that now goes by the name IMX, but in my day, they were Immature.[2] Pre-2003, my boy band addiction led me to become a wary observer of all things Internet. My high school friend Vuyo had a PC at home with dial-up internet. She didn't live in a township (like me) and her mom was cool enough to know that internet access was more than a business expenditure.

When her mom was working late or out with friends, we would put on our brave faces and venture into the world of fan chatrooms. This was the equivalent of sneaking out to attend a party that a much older boy invited you to. (Small sidebar: if you think the Beyhive is extra online, then you have not experienced American fans of a boy band in the early 2000s. The whole thing was like the WWF before it became the WWE and the legitimacy of the performances was questioned.) Vuyo and I would never engage but observed fans verbally smack each other down about who their favourite band member was.

---

2 I know, right? Nineties bands had interestingly non-ironic names.

I was Team Batman and Romeo and Vuyo was an LBD girl.[3] The chaos reassured me that I wasn't missing anything by not having internet access at home. My dad was right — only legitimate businesses needed it. Besides, loading a single page took so long (yep) and cost so much that I was not willing to risk my role as my father's favourite child for a glimpse into fan mania.

In 2002, my parents shipped me off to university in Grahamstown, a ten-hour drive away in a different province. My home was still an internet-free zone so I wasn't expecting things to be drastically different at university. My naïve expectations evaporated when I realised that I could not get through my three years of university without at least getting to know a PC.

Most of my classmates and a few girls at my all-girls residence had their own PCs (what in the Bill Gates had my parents gotten me into?). I had to use one of the university's public computer labs that came equipped with PCs, printers, and a lab assistant who was a low-level problem solver. Unfortunately, the lab assistant couldn't spare the time to teach me how to use a computer, so I had to find a Mr Miyagi.[4]

I randomly picked the Jac Labs where I "waxed on and off" (not a sex thing) until I had a Hotmail account and dared to

---

3 I wish I could explain these intricacies, but none of it matters now. Just know that the three group members were Batman, Romeo, and LBD, and fans were willing to suplex each other for days over their favourite group member.

4 A character from a 1984 film called The Karate Kid. Mr Miyagi helps an awkward whiny boy who is getting bullied by teaching him Karate. He spends 70 percent of the movie getting the kid to do housework and handyman jobs. I know … 80s movies were very weird. Watch it anyway.

visit a few chatrooms as a spectator. It took me a good few months to finally join the conversation. Once again, I was out of my depth, but being a late bloomer has taught me to fake it until you make it.

While Zuckerberg was working on The Facebook, I too was working on an important project: understanding Internet Lingo. I couldn't admit to my friends that I was Internet Illiterate so there was no way I could ask them to decode the language of my Miyagi Training. ASL? That was what people asked when you joined the conversation in a chatroom. Lab Assistant to the rescue? Nope. One quiet night in the labs, when I was supposed to be working on an essay, I made eye contact with the Lab Assistant. He did not look, as MCU Thor once said, "to be in a gaming mood." So I turned to the nerd next to me: "Pssst, what the hell is ASL?" Without looking up from his screen, he shouted, "Age, sex, location!" With those three words, I entered the world of chatrooms, and boy did I spend a lot of time "completing Linguistics assignments" at the Jac Labs after that.

University was difficult for me. On the outside, it seemed like I was having a good time with my friends, but something was eating away at me. In retrospect, I name the parasite depression, but back then I felt like I didn't fit in anywhere. Online, though, I was part of something new and wonderful with friends from all over the world. I didn't have to worry about wearing a heavy smile to hide my real feelings. My internet friends and I gathered in the Jac Labs on my computer screen and spoke about everything and nothing. We had inside jokes and often asked where X was if they were missing from our gatherings. It was admittedly like having a conversation with twenty people in a loud bar — there were too many conversations happening at once. This wasn't a problem until I started craving privacy with one member of a particular chatroom.

Inevitably, I started an online flirtation with a Matt with several numbers behind his name. I kept him to myself and we emailed religiously. It didn't seem that odd because one of my high school friends had found love on the internet a few years earlier. She used to print out their communications to share with us.[5] Matt-Numbers and I spoke in the chatrooms and privately. I could sense that he was eventually going to ask for more. He was in Johannesburg, the place I called home, and I was a ten-hour drive away in Grahamstown. Full disclosure: I was also busy with real-life boys. (I was a late bloomer, not a nun.) Real-life boys were fun but stupid, and Matt-Numbers really understood me. The days where I couldn't manage a smile or a teary phone call with my best friend, I sat in the Jac Labs and received <3 and :) from an intimate stranger. Yes, yes, Matt-Numbers could have very well been an older man who was hoping to lure me out of the computer and kidnap me. I'm aware. That, however, did not stop me from agreeing to meet him during the Easter holidays.[6]

In the run-up to the Easter break, cold feet and common sense set in. Matt-Numbers had only seen two photos of me even though he sent me many of himself. Why did that not bother him? He knew a lot about my loneliness. Why was I an oversharing mess? What the hell was I going to tell my parents?

---

5 No screen grabs back in our day — you had to commit to killing an entire forest if you wanted to boast about your relationship.

6 I can already hear my friends saying "Jesus did not die for this."

What was I thinking? Besides not being able to communicate with Matt-Numbers while I was at home — my father's beliefs about who needed internet access hadn't changed — I was catching up with friends I hadn't seen in months. The guilt of standing up Matt-Numbers washed away over days in malls, bars, and restaurants with friends. But sometimes when I was with my real-life friends, I would make a reference that only my chatroom pals would get. That was the first time it started feeling like I had a double life.

I waited until I got back to university, after Easter break, to communicate with Matt-Numbers. Internet cafes existed, but it was too much trouble to leave Soweto and drive around looking for one in town, all so I could explain why I wasn't meeting a person I knew but didn't know at all. Matt-Numbers had sent me three emails and then I suppose he gave up. My apology emails went unanswered, but it wasn't a total loss. The end of my relationship with Matt-Numbers coincided with graduation and the end of my days in the Jac Labs. My Miyagi internet training was over and I was ready for whatever came next.

In 2005, I moved to Cape Town to study for a post-grad diploma. A friend found a place that we ended up sharing with two fresh-out-of-high-school boys. Everybody had a PC, except me. My dad didn't see why I needed one, so I often used my friend's for any assignments. While I was slumming it in Cape Town, back home in Soweto, my father had a work laptop AND my younger brother had his own PC. The excuse was that "he needed it for school." He was in high school, but I studied for a degree without one. Last-born children get all the nice things!

Studying during the day and waitressing at night took up all my time, so I couldn't stay in touch with my chatroom friends. Breakups affected dynamics, we outgrew each other, life did its thing, and a few moved on to better things. MySpace was one of those "better" things. You could make your profile as obnoxious and sparkly as you wanted, and you already felt cool because you started with one follower. Tom from MySpace made us unpopular, impressionable young types feel good about our presence on the site. MySpace was like a business card for us. You could come across random people, and they could see what you were about from your profile (which is how I found fellow music lovers and creators). You could also tell your friends, colleagues, acquaintances, and a few people you hooked up with to follow you on MySpace.[7]

But MySpace lacked that community vibe. I posted a few blogs and eventually gave up; it felt like shouting into the void. You must understand my Miyagi Years on the internet consisted of waiting a long time for a photo to load. My friend had a digital camera and we used to save all our photos on a disc. We had none of this saving memes and adding one to every tweet — we worked hard for our uploading and downloading of photos. But times changed: internet connections improved (in some places) and people started posting lots of photos of themselves. When I did drop in, I noticed that photos had changed the way people interacted. The beautiful guys and girls gained popularity; the unsigned singers amassed followings because the space wasn't saturated. (Well, we thought it was, but Zuckerberg had plans for us *evil laugh*.) Truth

---

7 Only the ones with good taste in music, of course.

is, I didn't have a PC and when I did, internet connection in Soweto was infuriatingly slow. I couldn't fully immerse myself in the experience. Again, I felt left behind.

A year later, when I was working in advertising, a colleague told me about Facebook. She said it was the best way to stay in touch with people and all you needed was an email address and to swear you weren't a toddler. Seemed easy enough. Except it was like an unrequested family and school reunion with people poking you and pretending to be farmers (whatever happened to Farmville?). Facebook was too grown up and I preferred to focus on my after-hours music career. (Keep up, I've lived a million lives.[8])

With music taking up a lot of my life, I started following music blogs. I eventually started my own and belonged to a small group of Blogspot folks who cheered each other on and left a million comments on every post. My favourite part of this experience was discovering new musicians. I spent time on my newly acquired laptop and home internet just searching for fresh content. Through my Blogspot crew, I discovered a singer-songwriter and rapper from the UK. She was sharp, talented, and just a joy to follow. We all shared our collective excitement when she moved to the US to work with John Legend. Her huge hit "American Boy" (featuring Kanye West) made us all feel like a proud family. Estelle inspired

---

8 Just a few of the things I've dabbled in: singing waitress, radio producer, radio presenter, client services at an advertising agency, street performer, music video actor (in my childhood), voice over artist, record label owner, scriptwriter for e-learning videos, MC at national award show, etc.

me to keep making music. Who says internet connections are not productive?[9]

My blogging slowed down until I was only posting once every two weeks. Hosting a radio show and performing my music in the evenings meant I spent my down time with friends or napping. The Karate Kid (go along with this messy metaphor) was feeling like a veteran. What could possibly come next? Was my Internet Youth over? Was I doomed to being a Facebook adult or Farmville farmer forever? My cool early adopter friend Luana enters Stage Left. "Why are you not on Twitter?" she asks. It's 2009 and I'm still wary of new things. "What on earth is Twitter?"

I signed up and found myself wondering what kind of mess Luana got me into. I could only see her tweets and I learned TWO WEEKS later than RT did not stand for Reply To. All the cool kids knew what they were doing, so I decided to fake it until I understood what was going on. In 2010, I knew I had made it, because I had a small group of Twitter users who included me in their good morning, goodnight, and Follow Friday tweets. Woohoo! I was once again leading a double life, except I was no longer a frightened and depressed nineteen-year-old. I was an independent Sowetan in her early twenties, living in Cape Town. I had made it through smack down cha-trooms and MySpace duckface phases, and my early internet experiences had given me parts of myself I didn't know existed. You could say I was becoming *more* myself. Also, life isn't as frightening when you're not depressed.

I still wasn't sure about tweet-ups — stranger danger — but I did finally agree to meet a small group of my favourite Tweeps

---

9 *My father.*

(yes, we called each other that). We hit it off immediately! The wine was flowing and so was the conversation. These people weren't far away; like my previous online pals, they were in the same city as me. We were building an online and real-life community. It was at this point when it felt like my two worlds had merged. I was an adult who met people on the internet and it wasn't unheard of. My online and IRL life friends met and I created brand new communities for myself. My life was becoming bigger and richer.

I met some of my very good friends on Twitter. Amanda went from being a face next to a tweet to being one of my best friends. I met her son when he was in prep school and he's now in high school. We all remember her eldest child's first day of high school — that young person is almost ready to graduate from university. Fellow *Doctor Who* lovers sent me photos when they ran into Jodi Whittaker in Cape Town. When I had time to kill, I would send out a "Who is in town and wants to have a drink?" message, knowing that someone I knew would show up and we could chat. (I don't do that anymore because my friends, some of whom I met on the internet, say it's not safe — real stranger danger!) Twitter and real-life friend Liam moved to Dubai, then came back to Cape Town. While he was away, we stayed in touch on Twitter more than over the phone. When I started writing for comic books, I followed a bunch of creators and lovers of comics.

It's so easy to feel alone when you're living between worlds — I am a code-switching girl from Soweto who was constantly being thrust into new experiences in a new South Africa. The assimilation process for black South Africans my age was something completely new; we had nobody to run to when we were confused, alone, or tired. We lived double lives and didn't even know it — there was School Me and Home Me. In retrospect I can see why the internet had so much appeal — it was the one place where I could be Me Me.[10] Without sounding like a character on *X-Files*, there were others out there just like me.

While my eight-year-old nephew grew up with the internet all around him, I found pieces of myself all around the internet. Chatrooms helped me be comfortable with myself and my weird sense of humour. While those connections may not have been everlasting, I kept at it. My house is often filled with the voices of people who were once just userpics online. Exercising my internal voice online transformed how I communicate with family and friends — if I can tell strangers online how I feel, I should be able to tell those close to me. Many years after I joined Twitter, I was able to tell my parents about my mental illness. My online friends knew about it before they did. There was a real fear of rejection or not being understood by those close to me, but they supported me in a way that surprised and softened me.

It is funny how I went from the child of a man who didn't think we needed a PC or internet access at home to the adult daughter of a man who ghost-follows me on Twitter and emails me once a week. So much has changed it's like I've almost forgotten those early days of IMX fans with their verbal smackdowns. But here I am: once a late bloomer, now a grumpy Internet Aunty who reports trolls and wishes people were kinder to each other on Twitter.

---

10 Hehe. Meme.

Speaking of being kinder, a part of me feels like I should apologise to Matt-Numbers[11] because rejection sucks! If it makes any difference, Matt-Numbers, I grew up to be an adult who willingly meets guys IRL via Tinder. Our timing was just off, I'm afraid.

---

11 *This apology only applies if Matt-Numbers was a real boy and not some creepy old man.*

UNDER THE LJ-CUT:
A LOVE STORY

Lola Keeley and Kaite Welsh

There's a generic avatar, a presumably fake name, and just enough personal information to get a sense of who this man is. He's a blank canvas, there only to have our hopes and dreams projected onto him. This list of facts and figures is the back-story to the raw material we need to make a baby, an entire human reduced to physical features we'll probably never verify in person, and a list of interests that have to stand in for a full personality.

Which was a lot like our starting point for finding a wife, it turns out. Only then it was clicking on the mutual inter-ests — Candice Bergen, political satire, and autumn — in our LiveJournal profiles instead of shopping for sperm donors in what seems like an endless online IKEA catalogue of tall, handsome, well-educated men. Among early adopter late mil-lennials, LiveJournal became shorthand for a certain type of introspection, a place where outcasts and misfits would chronicle their adventures in mental health, music, and 100x100 pixel user icons.

Before we had a shared futon, a joint tenancy agreement, or any of what would become a menagerie of cats, we had LiveJournal.

First impressions matter, regardless of platform, and for a while we were only a header banner of Kristin Scott Thomas' breasts communicating with an icon of Captain Janeway, mostly about a mutual love of showtunes. We orbited each other the way people did back then, in comments and friends-only filters, picking up stray facts about one another without ever really engaging. Lola dreamed up six different pronunciations of Kaite, never once guessing it was literally "Kate with an i for no good reason." It was easy for Kaite to mentally tack on about five years to Lola's age, simply because she had a real job and expensive sunglasses.

We could have gone on like that quite happily, dating people who were not each other and occasionally leaving a sympathetic comment about a hellish commute or looming exam. And then Lola's best friend Lis spoiled everything.

Lola was coming up to Edinburgh on a work trip from London but Lis was busy — could Kaite meet Lola for a coffee until she was finished? As it happened, the work trip was cancelled, and that could have been the end of it had it not been for Lola's fiendish plot. You see, while Kaite was going happily about her life, writing *Buffy the Vampire Slayer* fanfic, practising witchcraft, and going to lectures, Lola had a Machiavellian plan that would not be revealed for another sixteen and a half years, during the writing of this very essay. She had every intention of coming up to Edinburgh and seducing Kaite with her soft butch wiles for one torrid weekend before loving and leaving her.

Nice try, darling.

A quick message over MSN Messenger turned into a two-hour conversation that led to the first of many missed appointments, preferring each other's digital company to Celtic Civilisation lectures or whatever Lola was supposed to be doing. Work, presumably.

Now, this was long before Tinder was just a glint in an app developer's eye, long before apps were even a thing. Back in 2003, according to our parents, everyone on the internet was almost definitely a serial killer and any personal information you let slip was a direct route to death, dismemberment, and your photograph featuring prominently on *Crimewatch*.

But even potential serial killers deserve love, and since we had at least one person in common to verify that we were both who we said we were, we eventually met in person at an Ani DiFranco concert with Lis in tow (remember — this was 2003 and we're lesbians. We did that sort of thing back then). After months of MSN messaging, constant texts, and even daily phone calls, we'd shared enough that we weren't really meeting for the first time. Not to sound like nymphomaniac hipsters, but we were sexting before it was cool (although not during the concert, because in those days people had goddamn *manners*). It was also much more expensive at 10p a text, but it was an investment that's more than paid off.

Even once we were officially together, most of our relationship happened online by necessity. The four hundred miles between London and Edinburgh remained a thorn in our mutual side, and to this day, we have an irrational loathing of Peterborough, just for being on that train line. The payoff for a long-distance relationship, though, is that eventually you end up in the same place. What we weren't prepared for was how much the parting each time was going to hurt. The cheeky texts and sappy comments that sustained you just a week before seemed hollow after actually getting to be in the same room. A well-chosen avatar was no comparison to seeing a raised eyebrow in person. And after being able to kiss, and touch, and . . . well, you get the picture. It was shockingly difficult to go back to being disembodied words on a screen after that.

That led to some seriously angsty conversations, even when we were in that first flush of happiness. Geography was our nemesis, and time a sneaky thief. We braved ten-hour bus journeys because they were the cheapest option, and that meant more chances to be together. But then one of us would have to make the return trip, which led to unprecedented public displays of emotion, right down to a sobbing Lola reenacting the *Shawshank Redemption* by falling to her knees in the rain right outside Victoria Coach Station.

But where could two women in their early twenties brimming with love, lust, and relatable song lyrics possibly go to share those feelings at considerable, barely edited length? That's right, we kept it all right there on LiveJournal, the last great long-form blogging platform.

The beauty of LiveJournal was its privacy. Locked entries, filters to manage different levels of access depending on the person, and the ability to temporarily delete the whole thing should an appropriate fit of pique occur. The sanctity of the confessional had nothing on the integrity of the LJ friends-lock. If that little padlock was in evidence, then the content of the post went no further.

To grant someone access to everything was about more than just trust — it was the online equivalent of standing there naked and saying "this is me," like something out of an anxiety dream set in your school cafeteria. Transparency with another person was the grandest of gestures.

Until things weren't going so well. When petty annoyances became regular enough to warrant their own filter. A select group to provide advice on minor relationship issues that started blowing up into major ones. In retrospect, those were growing pains for a relationship started when we were both barely twenty. In real time, using filters that excluded each other felt like more of a betrayal. When we broke up, our online friends knew before we told each other, but damn if that *omertà* wasn't completely watertight.

Which meant that the messy fallout of those breakups was chronicled there as well, with our overlapping friends list reading both sides, occupying the space between voyeur and child of divorce. You don't make it to sixteen years and counting without breaking a few eggs, but there's something to be said for having the fights and imagined slights a few clicks away at all times.

The first one was four months in. Edinburgh to London was one thing, but when Lola's new job promised to take her further afield, the writing was on the wall. Despite the heartbreak and occasional outbursts of passive aggression that follow any breakup, we both had a lovely time — and although we secretly missed each other, neither of us would admit it. A waitress in Bogota here, a burlesque dancer with a snake tattoo from shoulder to ankle there. A Shakespearean comedy of errors where Lola, for one long and terrible moment, thought Kaite had slept with Lis, all culminating in flirting wildly in the restaurant where we had our third date and both completely ignoring the birthday girl — the ever-patient Lis — on the other end of the table and the girlfriend back in Edinburgh, then refusing to speak for months.

A cold — or at least, distinctly lukewarm — war was broken after several months in a plot twist that would have made an audience roll their eyes so hard a team of optometrists couldn't save them. Kaite, feeling vaguely melancholy and nostalgic during a rare quiet night tending bar in a tourist trap pub, thought she'd drop Lola a quick text to see how she was after her shift. Maybe admit she missed her, maybe not. Turning her phone on, lo and behold, there was a message from Lola saying just that. History repeated itself — texting turned to a phone call, and by the time the sky started to lighten, Lola was moving up to Edinburgh and we were back on.

There were hiccups in the intervening years, breakup posts written and then deleted, sometimes in the space of a day, sometimes a week. Luckily for us, the last of those breakups was back in 2009. We were reunited within six months, engaged four more after that. To this day there are probably still friends permanently braced for the next instalment of drama, even though our last fight was about Kaite's slapdash approach to putting the bin liner in the kitchen bin. And maybe that's one of the reasons our blogging habits fell by the wayside — who wants to read about domesticity?

At the same time, LiveJournal was having some makeup and breakup issues of its own, changing hands and radically changing policies with it. Our personal happiness overlapped with a little something known as "strikethrough," in which our new Russian overlords started wiping out journals and communities for having even a whiff of anything L, G, B, or T about them. Years of discourse, memories, and just plain fun were obliterated without much by way of appeal.

People fled the platform like ships deserting a sinking rat, to Dreamwidth and a few other short-lived experiments. By then we had been sucked into the MySpace-Facebook-Twitter production line for a decade of unexpected autoplay and in plenty of time for fake news. Now instead of going instantly to the "post new entry" screen, our personal news was finally being shared with actual family members, friends we regularly had drinks with, and a disturbing number of people we went to high school with. Our LiveJournal friends, the ones whose real names we hadn't learned, who hadn't migrated with us to social media, were being left behind. There are people we were briefly but deeply close to who probably have no idea we got back together, let alone acquired so many cats.

We missed out, for the most part, on online dating the way we see it now. Aside from some truly terrible GaydarGirls dates — one including both a missing tortoise and clown porn — there's a whole relationship style that's passed us by. We've never swiped right on each other — had Tinder been around we might never have met, since left and right are things Kaite still has to think about and look down at her hands to check. We've never slid into each other's DMs. It has drastically reduced the number of dick pics we get sent in comparison to our friends, so that's an upside.

What we got instead was something with much more of a shelf life, deepening and improving as the years ticked past. After our wedding in New York, at City Hall, we met with friends to raise a glass and officially celebrate the elopement. Every person at that table, with a glass of bubbly in hand, had made the journey with one or both of us from usernames to real names, and from avatars to much-beloved faces in their own right.

When we decamped to the Stonewall Inn, commemorating the newly passed same-sex marriage laws that had allowed us to get hitched in the first place, it was with a merry troupe that included friends we'd bonded with over the impact of an Aaron Sorkin walk-and-talk, others still who'd been co-conspirators in driving the moderators of the *bwaydaily* community completely insane. There was the friend from a musical theatre Yahoo! Group who became Lola's *de facto* sister and the writer whose early blog posts Kaite can still quote by heart. Even now we're still in touch, although we're as likely to be comparing notes on mortgage rates as we are to be tweeting about all the intersections of our tastes and fandom, or tagging each other on Facebook about some old joke whose punchline we've never quite forgotten, even though the rest of the joke eludes us.

Oversharing is a hard habit to break, but these days the internet is more public, our relationship more private. You can glean a lot from our Tumblr tags for each other, not least that Kaite really likes dinosaurs (but not in that way), but the days where every disagreement or niggling doubt was analysed online have gone. So often the first person we want to tag or rope into that day's nonsense will be each other. It doesn't take long on either of our feeds to work out that in many ways we come as a package deal, even with our very distinct creative genres and wildly diverging tastes. In some ways we use the internet differently and in some it will always be the same, patterns formed when our online social circles were smaller and our real names kept far away from our usernames.

These days, Kaite journals about tarot cards and horoscopes on Dreamwidth and Lola posts fanfic on Tumblr. The interests haven't changed as much as the platforms have, and perhaps we're still searching for something that feels like our first online community, chasing the dragon of connection through anonymity. The time invested has certainly shrunk, not least because our attention is being pulled in fifteen directions that didn't exist when we poured our hearts and souls (or at least our bad moods) into a daily LiveJournal update.

It's only going to reduce further when the Scandinavian sperm shopping finally pays off, preferably before Brexit pushes up the shipping costs. With crossed fingers and hopefully uncrossed Fallopian tubes, at some future date we hope to be welcoming a baby into our lives, more offline than on. Maybe by that point we'll be too exhausted to think about it, but a little part of our brains is still programmed to wonder what witty tag we'd use for posts about the baby, or which dropdown menu mood embodied by a pixellated purple cat would fully capture the pre-emoji reaction to their arrival.

LiveJournal is still live, and indeed our journals are still hosted on there, even if they're all locked down and downloaded as archives for the inevitable day when it all comes tumbling down for good. All it takes now is a click on what we used to call our "flist" (friends' list) to see the tumbleweeds, the lack of new content and interaction from something that was our daily hub of online socialising. A few communities are still running, and of course there's plenty of spam, but the broader community has evaporated, lost to an internet that most of us using it today wouldn't even recognise.

But there's a romance to that. Maybe we had LiveJournal just as long as we needed it. A space to share and grow, to revel in drama and avoid the real world. To practice our writing and learn how to edit. If it's remembered for nothing else in the long run, for us it's always going to be the place we truly got to know the respective loves of our lives.

THIS IS NICE. NOW DO MORE.

Leah Reich

When Katie asked me if I wanted to write about the internet, I said yes without hesitating. And there was no question in my mind that I would write about Flickr. But when the time came to do the thing, to actually sit down and write, I realised how foolish I'd been. Not only because I'd taken on the task of describing, in words, the incredible photography and art featured on Flickr over the years — a picture is worth a thousand words, if you recall, not the other way around — but because I'd committed myself to talking about a community far bigger than my tiny part in it. What if I failed to honour it? What if someone from that time read it and remembered it, or worse, remembered me, differently?

More than all of that, I'd committed to something that, after many years of deep self-examination and painful, intentional change, I still am not comfortable doing. I'd committed to publicly calling myself an artist. This essay isn't about a website. It's about a community that nurtured me and allowed me to become something I didn't think I was. Maybe it's something I still don't think I am. But the first draft of this essay was distant and hollow because I was too busy embodying my fears and what ifs, and too afraid to embody a simple truth.

Which is this: I am an artist.

For that I have Flickr to thank. It's hard to imagine there are people who don't know what Flickr is, mostly because Flickr looms so large in my own online landscape. It's like having to explain to someone what the Empire State Building is when all you've ever known is the New York skyline. Flickr was, or rather still is, a photo hosting website, one that emerged in the early 2000s as a way for people to upload pictures, share them with friends, post them to blogs. For all I know, it still has pockets of people engaging and commenting and exploring one another's photos. I never gave up my account, so I could find out for myself. But whenever I try, it feels like visiting a town after the rapture. Most things are just where we left them, but the community I know isn't there. And that community, that's really what Flickr was.

I joined Flickr in 2005. I used it for a few years, mostly so I had somewhere to store and share photos. I wasn't taking many then, and the photos I did take were mostly snapshots. At some point, around 2007, inspired by the food blogs I was reading and the food I was making, I started taking photos of food and posting them to my own short-lived blog. My pictures were fine, but I wanted them to be great. I wanted them to be as good as the photos on blogs I loved, like Molly Wizenberg's Orangette. Her photography was quiet but so rich with stories and textured moments — people eating dinner shot from above, stills of fruit and afternoon light on a white kitchen table. I wanted to be like Molly, with whom I'd become friends, so I tried to copy her. Inspired by her, I bought a Pentax K1000 SE. I'd never had a 35mm camera of my own, only point-and-shoot cameras in the 1980s and 1990s. Molly, an avid Polaroid shooter, also gifted me a Polaroid Spectra camera. I went out, armed with my new tools, and tried to capture what I'd seen Molly capture. My early pictures were somewhere between my pre-adolescent snapshots and the art student phase I never had. They were fine, at best. I loved them anyway, because I felt a real joy in taking them and sharing them on Flickr. Even so, I wanted them to be better than fine. I wanted them to be good.

One of the things that made Flickr so special was that it was intentional about community. Rather than let toxic culture take root, the company as well as the users thought about what kind of culture they wanted, and they worked to make sure that culture thrived. There were community rules that were enforced, and often there were in-depth discussions and heated debates about those rules, which shifted and changed as the community did. There was the feeling that we were all responsible for the community and the culture, both creating them and protecting them. Maybe we didn't yet know how toxic online culture could be, but we did know that we had something special, and that it was up to us to help keep it that way.

Flickr, like many vibrant, creative communities, was diverse in its populace and in its interests. Not everyone did the same kind of work, but we found ways to connect with each other just the same. There were groups dedicated to different kinds of photography, different cameras, different photography-related activities. All sorts of people from around the world started commenting on my pictures, and I commented on theirs. We were supportive, even when the photography wasn't that great. Commenters offered constructive criticism and suggestions about how to improve, what worked and what didn't, what sorts of tools and techniques to consider. Those people kept coming back, and our comments progressed from polite, friendly chatter to something much deeper, much funnier, much more heartfelt.

One of the most well-known activities that people engaged in on Flickr was the 365 Project. It has a deceptively simple conceit: You take a picture every day for a year, and you post it online. Some people took it a step further with a 365 Self-Portrait Project — we still called them self-portraits, before selfie became a word and then a phenomenon. While I did a lot of self-portraiture at the time, I decided to do a regular 365 Project. One photo every day. It's harder than you think. Maybe nothing interesting happens, and you have to find something in the nothingness. Maybe one day you forget until 11 p.m., just before bed.

Or maybe it's a terrible, devastating day, like the day I had to put my beloved fifteen-year-old cat to sleep. I still took a picture that day, one that remains a favourite. I took it in the moments after I kissed my cat on the head one last time and the vet had carefully wrapped the small, lifeless body in a towel to take her out of the room. I sat there, alone, sobbing, unable to think. But something inside me knew I had to capture the moment, if only to do something and feel less helpless. A small part of me also knew, even in my grief, that if the photo came out despite the dim, yellow light in the exam room, it would be a good picture.

I would never have been able to take that photo without Flickr. It's astonishing to me that, in one year, I went from taking those first Polaroids to taking that picture of my crumpled tissues and the empty syringes on the exam table. It wasn't just that I knew there would be an outpouring of emotional support when I developed the film and posted it. It was also that my Flickr community had helped give me the confidence to trust in what I saw and felt, to heed the urge to create rather than second-guess or dismiss it outright. For years, it had been so natural for me to ignore whatever creative or artistic impulse I'd had by telling myself I wasn't skilled at visual arts, or that whatever I saw wasn't really creative. I got to rewrite that narrative by combining a daily practice with the feedback — sometimes supportive, sometimes critical — of people who genuinely wanted to help me improve.

Like my friend Kari. For the first hundred days of my 365 Project, I took those perfectly fine photos I'd been taking for the previous six months. People liked them, and I was having fun. And then on day 100 Kari commented, "This is nice. Now do more."

More! I knew what more was, at least in theory. More was in Kari's pictures of California landscapes and road signs, which simultaneously had a definite sense of place and an almost dreamlike quality, as if she had imagined them. Or in some of the photos featured so prominently in a group called the Female Self-Portrait Artists' Support group, photos that felt both grounded and otherworldly, that raised as many questions as they answered, and that maybe were for no one's benefit but the artist's. More. The only problem was that I didn't think I knew how to do more.

But I tried anyway. I thought about how Kari didn't just tell me to do more: She told me to do more because she believed I could. I respected and admired her so much that this belief was what I needed to believe in myself. I didn't let myself listen to fear, didn't let myself worry about what might happen if I tried and failed. I piled books onto a table, plopped my trusty Minolta Instant Pro on top of the makeshift tripod, and I took my first double exposure self-portrait.

Never in my life had I made something that, when I held it in my hand, matched what I had imagined in my head. I don't mean specifically in terms of technique, but more my vision. The feeling I wanted to convey, the imagery, the questions: They were all there in this single Polaroid. I posted it as day 101, and Kari loved it. So did everyone else.

I became known for my Polaroid self-portraiture, particularly the double exposure self-portraits. I wrote about them for a friend's book. A few years later I even had a show of self-portraits. All because of Flickr.

I should tell you about those self-portraits, because they were some of the last photographs I ever took in any serious sense, before I somehow stopped shooting and returned to my old narrative, the one in which I have no real artistic sense. But before I can tell you about them, I need you to know something else about Flickr that mattered just as much as my brief ability to believe in myself. Flickr people showed up for each other, and when I say showed up, I mean all the way. Like many communities, we had meetups and photo walks, and it was always wonderful to meet people whose lives you'd seen in their photos. But we also rallied for each other when life threw us challenges that no photo could successfully convey. People sent handmade gifts in the mail, like Sarah with her knitted shawls. When Jodi was diagnosed with rheumatoid arthritis and posted photos about her often painful experiences, as well as portraits of other people with autoimmune diseases, the community supported her and cheered her on. When Ashley fell hard down a flight of stairs and broke her tailbone, I coordinated care packages from around the world, full of handmade gifts, inside jokes, and packs of film to cheer her up. We travelled the world to visit each other. We just showed up, over and over.

Like in 2010, when my mother almost died from an aggressive cancer. My mother, who, in a matter of weeks, had gone from an unstoppable force of nature to a barely living ghost. She went into the hospital in June, less than two weeks after my birthday. Ashley was in town visiting me then, the same Ashley of the broken tailbone, who also happened to be my best friend. We'd met on Flickr, commenting politely at first on one another's Polaroids, me admiring the colour of the incredible orange glass vase she had (which she later sent me), her loving the picture of our family dog. Over time our friendship grew through jokes and real messages, each knowing we'd found a kindred spirit. When she decided to fly from Australia to California to visit me in 2009, it seemed insane but also totally normal, and from the second she got off the plane, it was as if we'd known each other all our lives. So when my mother was admitted to the hospital while Ashley was in town, it felt as if the universe had made sure my sister was there to support me when I needed it most.

Ashley wasn't the only one. In fact, my Flickr friends were among the people who supported me the most, even though most of them lived far from Northern California. Like Nathalie, who emailed me from the Netherlands every single day for weeks on end to check on me. And when I posted the few photographs I'd taken during that time to Flickr, my community responded powerfully. That year I couldn't allow myself to feel anything, because I was afraid that letting feelings through would destroy me and keep me from moving forward and caring for my mother. Emotions were a luxury I couldn't afford until much later. But I could take pictures. The pictures I took — of her hospital room, of her wig, of myself alone in rooms and often times literally in pieces — channelled everything I couldn't feel, say, or write. It was like the vet's exam room all over again, except, once again: More.

Those were the self-portraits that I showed. And those were the last photographs I took that I remember really caring about. At the time I blamed graduate school and the fact that I had to finally finish my dissertation, get my PhD, not distract myself with photography. Then I had to get a job, and then came the iPhone, and then came the old narrative again.

But you know what the real culprit was? Flickr slowly died. We all scattered, and many of us started to lose touch. Sure, we found each other on Facebook, Twitter, even Instagram, but it was never the same. I lost my community. I didn't realise until much later how much I needed it. Not just for the friendship, because I still have many of those friends. But for the way it encouraged and taught me both the techniques of photography and the finer, more difficult techniques of believing in myself. A community raises you, and it also raises you up. I can rediscover that belief, the belief that I could and can create. But without Flickr it will be a much lonelier and lengthier pursuit. No one can tell you that you're an artist, but it helps when they do.

THE MAGIC HOTEL

Kyle Cassidy

"Dear Magic Hotel . . . " Invoking this like a spell is how I began LiveJournal posts when I was looking for a place to stay somewhere far from where I lived while seeking fame, fortune, and adventure as a photographer and author. And when your books are travel books, as most of mine are, it means that you need to produce a lot of travel on spec. Without the Magic Hotel, it wouldn't have been possible for me. But, it turned out, the Magic Hotel was far more than just a free place to stay.

In his 1869 book, *The Innocents Abroad*, Mark Twain said, "Travel is fatal to prejudice, bigotry, and narrow-mindedness, and many of our people need it sorely on these accounts. Broad, wholesome, charitable views of men and things cannot be acquired by vegetating in one little corner of the earth all one's lifetime." Twain had hooked himself up with a travel company, spending a year touring the Middle East and Europe and having a series of adventures. *The Innocents Abroad* was Twain's most popular book during his lifetime, but it's largely overlooked today — sadly, for it has a lot to tell. But Twain's observation holds up to scrutiny. In a series of studies published in *Social Psychological and Personality Science* in 2014, Jiyin Cao of Northwestern University posed the question, "Does travel broaden the mind?" and they found that yes, "breadth of foreign experiences increases generalized trust." The more countries we visit, the more trusting we are of other people.

Travel is difficult, it's time consuming, and if it's not time consuming, it's expensive, so we mostly don't do it. Where I'm from, people live and work and marry and die pretty much all in the same place — they've grown homogenous and isolated. My ancestors came here in the middle of the 19th century, fleeing a famine. They settled down on the east coast of the United States, and between them and me, the only two people who went more than a hundred miles from the place they were born were my great-great-great grandfather, James, who fought in the Civil War, and my father, who fought in Vietnam. I was fairly doomed to follow in my family's non-footsteps and never leave the small, rural, New Jersey town I called home.

But when the internet arrived, the world opened. Suddenly things got global — you could talk about motorcycles with people in Australia as easily as argue with your next-door neighbour about zoning for a new liquor store. There was so much promise and it woke me up. I didn't want to stay in the peach orchards of New Jersey. I wanted to see these places and meet these people from the Land of the Internet. I knew then I wanted to travel, but I didn't have the money. It seems a cruel fate of growing up that when you have time, you don't have money, and when you have money, you don't have time.

I'm sleeping on a living room floor in Woonsocket, Rhode Island, still a day's drive from where I need to be the next day. I wasn't planning on staying here, but the roads are flooded and the Magic Hotel coughed this up quickly. It's actually the softest, most plush carpet I've ever felt. It's like laying on a fifteen-foot-square sponge in this tiny one-story ranch house with a red exterior and a backyard full of flowers and trees you could fit a baseball diamond in. My assistant, Phil, is here too, laying on his back with his head resting on a pile of rolled-up clothes and a gigantic grey cat named All Ball sitting on his chest, staring into his eyes like he's waiting for a mouse to come out of a hole. Jeff and Stephanie, the people who live here, are out in the garage carving up the carcass of a deer they just brought home. He's a cop. Someone ran the deer over about an hour ago — he was dispatched to the accident and called Stephanie to come out and get the dead deer. I wake up at four in the morning to go to the bathroom. They're both in the kitchen, wrapping meat. We talk for a bit. They're both asleep when Phil and I wake up the next morning. We let ourselves out. All Ball stares at us through the window. Phil presses his hand up against the glass.

You can say "I want to travel" and feel a compulsion to visit places that are on the other side of the mountains. That's wanderlust. And you can say, "I want to see Yellowstone, and the grave of Edgar Allan Poe and Asheville, North Carolina" — those are just destinations. Just dreams, and even

together they might not get you out of town. With the Magic
Hotel, I had something that none of the people who had come
before me had: not just wanderlust, and not just destinations,
I had *havens*. And that gave me the ability to leave my house.
Perhaps it was being completely broke in college that's left
me thinking that a sofa, or even a floor, is a perfectly legitimate place to sleep — and after a place to store my luggage,
that's usually all I need. But the Magic Hotel was incapable
of delivering only that — it also provided social interaction,
pinpoints on a map where I could sleep, eat, charge batter-
ies, plan, access local knowledge, and glimpse into the life of
another human being. The Magic Hotel had everything, and
I had the Magic Hotel.

As a blogging platform, LiveJournal began in 1999, and
I found it in 2003. It's basically an online diary that you can
keep as public or as secret as you like, but it also allows you to
connect with people through communities which anybody can
create and to add people's journals to your daily reading list. It's
uncluttered, easy to navigate, and shows you every post your
friends have made in the order that they made them — which
seems like it's not a big ask or a remarkable feature, but it is one
of its most powerful aspects. Unlike Facebook, where the idea
seems to be to learn how horrible the people you went to high
school have become, the function of LiveJournal is to find and
connect with interesting people you don't know. LiveJournal
was doing things at the eking dawn of the 21st century that
Facebook has never been able to figure out — or more likely
hasn't cared to — and one of those things was foster community.
Without LiveJournal, the Magic Hotel likely wouldn't exist.
The Magic Hotel is a place that doesn't exist in the "real world"

or "cyberspace," but in the intimate, deep, origamic folds of community, like the vast, compacted coastline of a fjord — the closer you approach, the larger and more complex it becomes.

"Dear Magic Hotel," I'd say in a post, "I'm looking for a sofa in Cleveland Portland Seattle Boston Bucharest Weehawken" — or anywhere else — and the wheels of the internet would grind a little and invariably within a few hours, or even minutes, the Magic Hotel would answer: "I live two miles outside of Weehawken, we have a guest bedroom and a bicycle you can borrow." Almost always these offers came from people I didn't know and had never met who had been reading my blog for some time and were perfectly happy to open their homes and their lives to an Itinerant Adventurer. Apart from being a financial relief, it's a much better way to understand the places you're visiting. How much of the world can you see from a hotel that looks like every other hotel that you've ever stayed in? It may be sacrilege to say, but I tend to never visit museums when I travel. A museum is a collection of things from someplace you're not visiting. We've got an Hieronymus Bosch in Philadelphia. If I go to Germany, I'm not going to visit *St. John the Evangelist on Patmos* — I'm more interested in how people do their laundry. People are my mystery.

I think a lot of times that people live in the places they do because they don't know that being anywhere else would be much different, or better. You can see another place with much more clarity than your own home. You can travel to the most banal Other Place and say, "I am not from here," which is one thing that makes travel writing easier. You walk down your block every day, but you don't know the name of the trees and you haven't eaten at all the restaurants and you've never read the guidebook to your hometown. "Sometimes it is good to see your own country through the eyes of a tourist," Yannis, an internet friend from the Magic Hotel, told me in Bucharest after I had marvelled at the ruined architecture, stretching across the landscape like a thousand acropolises piled one upon the other. For me, it was a magic place; for him, it was an eyesore.

In the Sonoran Desert it's 110 degrees and the air is still and hot and like a hair dryer. We'd stopped the car along the side of the road because every mile or so there would be a giant sign that said "DANGER BEES" and I wanted to figure out how they could know where the bees were enough to put a permanent sign up.

There were bees — a great cloud of them swarming like electrons around the nucleus of a cylindrical pool of water. They'd swoop down and touch the surface, picking up tiny droplets and flying off in an imprecise wave, drinking in the heat.

On the side of the concrete bunker was spray-painted "RADIATOR WATER ONLY, DO NOT DRINK" — out here in the desert, everything is measured by its proximity to water; water is the thing that keeps you alive and its absence is the thing that kills you. And not just you, every living thing. Hence the bees. They swarmed the radiator water, disregarding the sign — they couldn't read and radiator water was better than no water.

It's 247 miles to a sofa in Phoenix.

The first rule of crowdsourcing is that you need a crowd. This can seem harder to grasp for some than you might think. I've seen a lot of people who should know better struggle with understanding how an interconnected world works. I've worked with advertisers whose marketing plan is "1) Produce product 2) It goes viral . . . ." The Magic Hotel, and everything else powered by the will of crowds, exists partly because of social media, but only in the way that a swimming pool exists because of a hole in the ground. For this to work, you have to be interesting, you have to be kind (or at least well behaved), and you have to have something to offer. The thing that made the Magic Hotel more than a concept was that I had a skill that could usefully be shared in small increments, and I could, through the Magic Hotel, book one- or two-day photography workshops that would pay for my travel. I'd teach for two days, work on my book for two days, and at the same time *I'd have met sixteen people*, seen their portfolios, heard their stories, gone to the restaurants and the bars and the parks and places that those people went to — and I'd found a small home in a new place surrounded by new friends, and the satisfaction that I'd helped them grow in their art. Slowly turning internet relationships into IRL relationships has been incredibly important for me.

I've used the Magic Hotel to write a book about gun owners, one about tattoos, one about roller derby, one about science fiction writers, one about knitting, one about librarians, and one about payphones. Along the way I've photographed album covers and book jackets and little assignments that paid so terribly that the only way I could have done them was to not have to pay a hotel. This has allowed me to photograph things that I believe in rather than ones that would necessarily make money.

Each time the Magic Hotel has coughed up far more than just a place to stay, it has validated my faith in human kindness. LiveJournal, and the thousands of people it connected me with, allowed me to develop this nomadic existence where I could put my finger down anywhere on a map, any place I wanted to go, and ask the Magic Hotel to help make it happen. Not only would there be a place to sleep, but also the opportunity to do a weekend photo workshop or some other way to pay the bills. It was like a perpetual motion machine powered by love and creativity.

While teaching in Toronto once, I ran into another photographer at a restaurant. He'd won a Pulitzer Prize years before and was, obviously, an exceptional talent. We bumped into one another from time to time on assignments in the photo pits or at gallery openings. He told me that he was also in town teaching a photo workshop. His students were each paying a thousand dollars and they'd rented a house on the beach with a cook and a sommelier who came by every evening with wine pairings. My workshop cost a hundred dollars and I was sleeping on someone's sofa with an incontinent one-eared dog and a bossy tabby cat named Orange Crush. But our take-home was the same. What struck me wasn't that I was sleeping on a sofa and smelled like dog, but how much of everybody's money he was wasting not teaching photography. Through it all I wanted to get to the thing, not the things around the thing.

> In the shadow of the remnants of Mount Saint
> Helens, which looms, bent and hunched above us
> like a chewed loaf of bread that's been in the rain,
> I'm sitting in a hot tub with a schoolteacher and an

airplane pilot firing potatoes into a washtub from a
pneumatic cannon they built. There's an energetic
whumph and then a loud *POW!* with Batman punctu-
ation as the potato disintegrates into the back of the
washtub. There's no one around for miles but us and
Bigfoot. The schoolteacher is a chemist and after we
run out of potatoes, she uses a ball of thermite to fuse
all the change in my pocket into a giant lump of black-
ened metal. People have a performative aspect to
them while having new visitors — it is, after all, called
entertaining. After the thermite smoke clears, we lay
back and stare up into the sky, which is as black as a
velvet curtain with the Milky Way cracking it in half,
and we look for shooting stars. Later I go to sleep in
a guest bedroom on a futon piled with books and
laundry and just enough space for me to lay down.
I wake up late the next morning with a pillar of light
landing across my eyes and discover that my hosts
have already left for work — entrusting me with the
entirety of their home and possessions. I pack my
bags and carry them out through the cathedral of
pine trees to the car where I discover that they've left
me a packed lunch as a parting gift. I have a hundred
miles to drive.

I had the good fortune to be, for a time, an assistant of
Mary Ellen Mark — one of the world's greatest photographers.
I learned from her many things about photography which were
all applicable to life in general as well. While they took me a
long time to understand, they all seem simple now, and I've

gotten somewhat practiced in proffering her lessons for people in small, digestible chunks. One of the most important was, "Everything is easier if you have a guide." In journalism they call these people "fixers" — a local with contacts. An oil well springs a leak in Minot, North Dakota, and all the reporters in America descend on it and spend their days spinning their wheels, while the one journalist who knows a junior pipeline welder they can ask for introductions gets all the interviews. This personal, human connection is the antithesis of a hotel where everything is formulated, carefully crafted, to keep you *away* from other people — to insulate you from the local environment and keep you, as much as possible, in a hermetic bubble. It is, in fact, possible to travel from an office building in Philadelphia to a hotel in Paris and back without ever once leaving an enclosed space, without ever being *outside* and without ever interacting with a single person who is not paid to talk to you. The Magic Hotel, by its very nature, always guaranteed a unique, radiant experience, and a human who cared, at least a little, about what I was doing.

I'm in a treehouse in Boston thirty feet up off the ground — the bed juts out over the yard below surrounded by a glass dome that lets you look up into the sky or down at the ground a terrifying distance below. There's a short ladder that lets you climb out onto the roof and at midnight I do — and see all of Boston glowing around me like ten thousand orange fireflies. "All these people are home," I think. I open up my laptop and it automatically remembers the wifi password from the last time I was here, six months

ago. I've been traveling for a dozen hours and tomor-
row there is so much work to be done. I haul my bags
up into the treehouse with a rope and start working,
planning for the next day. Then I lay on my back and
look out through the dome at the sky and fall asleep.

We can spend our lives trying to avoid people — looking
for solitary experiences, sanitised of the previous occupants,
our hotel rooms reset to a sterile default — but life is not that.
Human life is other people; we are social animals. We have a
shared experience and consciousness and each thing we build
is just an addition to the things that have been built before.
We are all adding wings to one giant construction project. My
experiences in New Mexico are tacked on to Simone De Beau-
voir's, and to the photographs Ansel Adams took in Taos, and
Charles Bukowski's poems. It's a grand history of us all, carved
out in blog posts and Flickr.

I see, occasionally, a meme on the internet shaming people
for sitting in a room with one another, staring down at their
digital devices instead of speaking with each other. I've used my
digital devices to make and keep friends all over the world, far
removed from my (to paraphrase Thoreau) barn and hundred
acres; I've seen the world and met people different than myself;
I've found love and trust and companionship and goals and
collaboration. So rejoice in your digital device — it is a marvel
that can bring us a new world of global tolerance and understanding now that suddenly you can meet people, easily, from
anywhere in the world who will help you destroy stereotypes;
all you have to do is interact meaningfully. The internet used
to be a nicer place — the early years certainty felt safer and

more communal — but that doesn't mean you can't find and have meaningful experiences using it.

So go ahead and ignore the person sitting next to you on the bus; take out your phone, see the world and change it. Shamelessly make friends in Bucharest and Reykjavik and Portland and Kentucky, shamelessly text those friends, learn their ambitions and the names of their dogs, plan your revolution, but then visit — go, grow, learn, teach. You've got this technology — use it and find the friends you want, wherever they are. Book a guest bedroom in the Magic Hotel and make something beautiful — be proud when you have, ache while you're away, and make bold plans to return.

I'm in a pink 1950s vintage RV parked in the desert in Arizona. It's midnight but I can see for miles just by the light of the stars. There are more of them in the sky than I've ever seen before. Two coyotes walk past outside, oblivious to me. The RV is the guest house of a metalsmith who's invited me to photograph her daughter's roller derby team. "Let's have belly dancers and fire spinners" someone had suggested, and because there were belly dancers and fire spinners, the desert turned into a point of light and motion and sound, and any raven flying overhead would have circled once around to try to make sense of what was happening. While I'm there the metalsmith shows me how to make a ring, with fire and hammer, like a Nibelung. It melts, it hardens, I hammer and shape it, and when I get home, I put it on my girlfriend's finger and we get married.

I used to spend a lot of time worrying about leaving home and coming home, but I've realised this is my home. Every place that's let me stay and all the people that let me in and the dogs that shared their sofas and that break my heart a little when they're not there the next time. The Magic Hotel is my organic solution to an increasingly isolated world. It's my living room floor filled with a visiting roller derby team; it's a midnight snack in my kitchen with an out-of-town author who just got back, exhausted, from a book signing; it's a place that loves and suffers and gives and cries and looks for joy and adventure. It's friends in odd places you see for a day at a time as the needle skips over the record of your life, people who want nothing more than to be good, to do good, and share their journey through time with other people. It's people giving the easy comfort of their lives and the places they've built with their experiences and memories — it's such a small gift materially, but it's an enormous gift emotionally. It's the embodiment of what makes us social creatures — a shared experience, a trust, and a desire to be part of something greater.

I'm on a sofa in Toronto with an ancient, opinionated cat named Orange Crush whose fur is dry and wild like shag carpet. He drools when I pet him and relentlessly smashes his head into my chin when I stop. The one-eared dog died two years ago, his collar on the bookshelf across from the TV with a box of ashes, held shut with a tiny gold lock. I'm staying here for three days working on a book about payphones. There's a framed 8x10 photo on the wall from the workshop I taught here six years ago where we're all standing together, arms stretched into the sky in victory filled with the joy of each other's company. I look at all the faces in it and wonder if they're doing well. I'm five hundred miles from my house, but this place feels like home. Home is a place you keep coming back to. And here the sofa smells familiar, my laptop remembers the wifi, and, like a home, the Magic Hotel is built out of love.

MONSIEUR THE MIDDLE MAN

Zuleka Randell Dauda

He was about six feet tall with a small head for his body and glasses with square frames. He used to sit on his balcony and speak French into his cellular device or work on his computer from his apartment next to a small portable radio on a wooden stool. He was serving with an international non-governmental organisation (INGO). He lived alone. I lived about three doors down with my family. I had to walk by his apartment every day while heading to and from school. I usually just greeted him or waved if he was on the phone. He was weird and creepy — and he was the only person I knew with an email account when I left Liberia.

Everyone just called him "Monsieur," but I would soon get to know his actual name. While living in Liberia, I never exchanged more than hellos and goodbyes with him, but Monsieur the stranger would become my lifeline to Liberia, a place I left due to civil war in hopes for a better life.

The early 2000s were my teen years, and I was ready to enjoy them until flying bullets altered my reality. Liberia was in yet another shamble of civil war and my family was forced to migrate to the United States. I arrived in the US in May when the school year was nearly over, so I had to wait to begin the following year. This meant a few months in the house with nothing to do while my immigrant mother worked overtime to get us settled into our new life. A girl can only watch so many *Kim Possible, Sister-Sister,* and *That's So Raven*s before she gets bored of seeing a life that does not reflect hers.

I missed my friends and family in Liberia. I missed the familiarity of a community, the people and the sense of belonging. I needed a medium to communicate with my friends and tell them all about my new life in America. I had to share with them my stories about greasy hamburgers, electricity that never went off, and of course white people that crossed the street when they saw Black people. The idea of race in America fascinated me; everyone was different, yet they pretended to be the same, even though they got treated differently! This new American world was way too captivating to keep to myself.

I had no source of income, but I needed funds to communicate with my friends. Occasionally, my mother gave me money for completing my chores: I just had to iron her uniform and I would have money to buy calling cards. I remember the calling card called BOSS. It had flags of various countries on it. They had $2, $5, or $10 cards on display at the Hispanic corner store. The $2 card only allowed me to call Liberia for eight minutes, so I would often get the $5 that lasted for twenty-five. When dialling, the excitement filled me up as I knew I would share stories with my friends on the other end. Unfortunately, most of my friends did not have their own phones at the time, so I had to wait for their parents or older siblings to get them. My calling minutes went by way too fast and I didn't get to talk about all my new experiences. Twenty-five minutes is only a long time when you are working out. I mean, even a sixty-second plank feels like eternity (I know I can't be alone with this!). In the middle of figuring out how to make my calling units last longer (I even wrote down some things to share before I made the calls), I remembered I had an email account!

The internet had hit Liberia in the early 2000s and I had felt the need to have an email account. I barely understood the intricacies of it all, but this was the thing to do, so I paid to get one. I opened my account only a few months before the war that drove me out. Since most of my close friends did not have email, I had to figure a way to get my email messages to them. But how?

The internet was still a luxury for many in Liberia. Most of my friends would have to pay to have access to the internet. First, one had to pay to open an account. Now, opening an account did not necessarily give you access. Access to the internet was commercialised by private suppliers in the form of internet cafés. Each time one attempted to access the internet, the most available option was the internet café, and that would mean paying a fee for a period of time, such as paying $100 Liberian dollars ($2.50 US) for twenty minutes of access. As a commercial venue, the strength of the internet also mattered, as connections were very slow and limited. At times, a person might only get half of the paid time with any useful access to the internet. Bear in mind also that Liberia was still in the midst of intermittent conflicts; the economy was not in good shape, and my friends did not have the kind of money they would need to keep in contact with me regularly.

And then I remembered Monsieur, my neighbour with internet access. Working with an INGO, Monsieur had uninterrupted access to the internet provided by his office, which was not the case for many in Liberia at the time (even most government agencies, private corporations, and businesses did not have internet). When I first got my email address, I had a little notebook that I collected email addresses in. It was a composition notebook with a black and white hard cover. I coloured in the white spots with markers to give it my teenage flare. Monsieur's email address was in there, but had .co instead of .com. I thought it was wrong, but I sent him a message the first week we got a computer in our home in the US. I tried both the .com and .co just to be sure:

> Hi,
> This is Randell your neighbour. I am in America now. How is Liberia? I really need to talk to my friends. Can you pass a message for me?

> *Hello Mademoiselle Randell,*
> *Happy to hear from you. How are you and America?*
> *Happy to share your message to your friends.*
> *What is it?*
> *Cheers, Monsieur*

Monsieur would print out my emails and give them to my friends. I imagined he would drive home in his big white Toyota

Land Cruiser with the INGO name printed in blue on the sides and Zoe would be waiting to receive my message.

> Hello Monsieur: hope you are okay. Please print this message for my friends. You can give it to Zoe and she will distribute to the rest of them. Thank you. Message: For Zoe — Girl! I can't believe I am typing this, but I am starting to like the food here. I know I said it is greasy and tasteless, but I am starting to get used to it. For Aminata — please tell all my other jolly-jolly partners hello for me. How's Kweeta? Oh and Mercy? Is she back in school na? What about Death Row? People still doing that? Hahaha I am excited to be here, but I miss you all. I wish I had a big net to just throw and catch all of you to come over the Atlantic. For Apulia — My bff, my lover, my everything!! You Geh, there are a million things to say. First, you need to hurry and open your email account. I have so much to tell you. I love you mehn. Please say hello to everyone.

The next day at school, Zoe would share the message with all my friends. They would gather their thoughts and responses and write me back, and Zoe would deliver the message to Monsieur. He would type it up and send it to me. This is how I got updates on their lives — my 2003 Facebook feed. I had to wait a lot longer to get them, but I was sharing my experiences and learning about what I was missing through this system we created with Monsieur at the centre. Over the next few months, we exchanged more than six hundred emails about my new life and what I was missing. Without Monsieur, I would have lost my entire network of friends.

My emails with Monsieur offered me a peek into life in Liberia. When I say peek, I mean really small, passed-on bits of information from the views of teenagers and Monsieur. Such realities include a friend who got pregnant as a teen. It was a huge scandal at school. I was there for that, but left shortly after the baby was born. I had to ask about her every chance I got, to hear about her whereabouts and the baby. I knew what happened to babies during the war. Being away also meant missing authentic Liberian food. I initially told Zoe I would never go a day without fufu (a starchy dish made to go with soup), but I later had to let her know I was getting used to eating burgers or fufu from the box. That was very important information to share with friends halfway across the world because they wanted to know how I was doing, just as I wanted to know their whereabouts, given the crisis in Liberia. Zoe needed to know I was going to be okay without real fufu, as the one in the box just doesn't do it! I was also the only girl in the all-male class group "Death Row," an after-school club named after the rap label Tupac was part of (Liberians copy a lot of American pop culture — it was very cool at the time, okay?). I had to communicate with the guys and tell them about my new guy friends. I needed to explain to my friends every day what I wore, what was cool, how people talk, girl drama — all the important teen things. We had a great chain of communication. I just didn't like the waiting part. I was hitting refresh every chance I got. I needed to hear from them, to know how they felt about the stories I shared. I was even more concerned about who wanted to kiss my then-boyfriend in my absence! I had so much to say with so little time, and no internet at their end. All I had to stay involved in the lives of my friends was my email exchange with Monsieur.

In America, I was fresh off the flight (because I came on a plane and not a boat, contrary to the ignorant "fresh off the boat" saying), and my mother had the brilliant idea for me to go to summer camp for high school debaters. In Vermont. What could go wrong attending summer camp in a new country, especially debate camp? I had to speak and make my points clear in front of people who constantly asked, "What did you say? I'm sorry, can you repeat that? What are you saying? Is that English?" I had to deal with the pressure of speaking in front of people like everyone else, but those questions really did something to my confidence. In Vermont I also encountered my first experience with racism — welcome to America! I was called a n*gger on the bus in downtown Burlington. I did not get mad because identity in America can be confusing. When that white old lady thought she was insulting me, I was actually learning. I do not feel the same about that word as other African-Americans. As a newly migrated Liberian, I did not understand the history of that word. I was just riding downtown to get a calling card so that I could talk to my friends. Another African-American/Black girl on the bus with me from New Jersey took serious offense and exchanged some really harsh words with the old lady. This was just my introduction to race and identity in America. I could go on about this issue, as it is really the uniform that we all wear whether we acknowledge it or not, but let me say that when given the choice to react to the way people see me, I always choose to just walk away. It is never about what they think I am, but who I know I am.

Someone please tell that white lady on that bus in downtown Burlington I am African and Bold!

The evening after the incident, I was anxious to share my experience with my friends, so I went back to my email to connect with my friends in Liberia. Sadly, the internet situation back home would not allow me to connect with them in real-time. So I emailed Monsieur about my experience in Vermont. I told him I didn't feel welcome and did not want to be there, but my mother had told me I needed to get used to unfamiliar places and try to fit in, as America was our new home. Monsieur told me we have to do things we don't want to do for people we love. I asked him to explain. He told me the woman he married was not his first choice for a wife as he wanted someone else. However, his culture and family made him marry not for love, but because it meant strong family connections with his wife's tribe. He did it mainly because his grandmother asked him to. She was his favourite and he wanted to please her and keep his family connections strong. He said, "Family is the greatest gift we have, so do what makes them happy." Although I was disappointed, I listened to Monsieur.

As much as the incident made me feel lonely and miss my friends, conditions in Liberia did not favour my return (war — duh!) and I was just trying to adjust. I did not understand why the colour of my skin made people treat me differently in America. This was never an issue growing up in Liberia. There, I did not know anyone from places I only saw on maps (Mauritius, Cape Verde, Puerto Rico, and many others), but America introduced me to these people. The internet was my line back to where I missed, but I did not want to return there. The civil war in 2003 was short but brutal, as were all of the ones previously. I do not remember much about the others, but 1996 had opened my eyes to the harsh realities of war. Leaving my friends behind in 2003 meant I could possibly never see them again. Every chance I got to talk to them or connect with them, I used it.

As Monsieur served at the centre of our network, he established his own relationship with me. Over time, we became friends through email. The creepy guy with glasses that I barely knew while living in Liberia would soon become my trusted confidant. Given our regular, if not daily, email exchanges, we went from just hellos and goodbyes to being almost family. In the time it took to get my friends to reply, he shared with me about his life and I did the same. Monsieur was from Liberia's neighbouring country, Côte d'Ivoire (Ivory Coast). He expressed his love for Liberian food, especially cassava leaves. He had left his family for a job with an INGO in Liberia mostly because he was miserable in his marriage. He was married to a woman almost two decades his junior. He was forty-two when we started communicating and she was twenty-two. At the time he spoke about her only as "Ma Femme" and I thought her name was Femme. It turned out that is just how you say "my wife" in French. In Liberia, we sometimes add Ma to older women's names as a sign of respect. This was not the case here. Monsieur and Ma Femme had three children, a boy and two girls, all under the age of three. We sometimes talked about them, but only briefly. I wondered if he missed them too much and that was why he avoided talking about them. Sometimes he only answered my questions about his family with, "Ehhh they are doing Ok!" I read into the short answers and exclamatory marks as "Let it be, Zuleka."

He would also compliment my fifteen-year-old body and it made me feel uncomfortable. I could have been reading into things, but his ways just seemed flirtatious to me. I debated asking him not to refer to me as "sexy thing," but I let that be, too. Monsieur confided in me that he was very unhappy with Ma Femme. He expressed his admiration for Liberian women as he told me his fantasies about waking up in another life with a Liberian wife. He told me he preferred big buttocks and his wife, Ma Femme, did not have that. Hearing a 42-year-old man tell me about his plans to touch girls felt like a secret only the internet could keep.

It is clear by now that Monsieur became a dear friend of mine and played a pivotal role in sustaining my relationship with friends back home in Liberia, but he did more than that. My conversations with Monsieur had turned into therapy sessions. I think sometimes I even found relief in just knowing I was not alone. I used to hurry back from school to check my email on the home desktop. Even when I didn't get replies from my friends, I knew without a doubt Monsieur would be there.

We talked about all sorts of topics through our emails. He wanted to know about American politics, so I started watching the news to share more with him. He would ask, "What is George Bush doing now?" and I would write what I remembered from the evening news. To my surprise, while watching one evening, I heard George W. Bush talk about the Liberian president at the time — Charles G. Taylor. I nearly jumped out of my seat. There was an order for him to step down from power in hopes that the war would cease. I spoke to Monsieur that evening and shared my feelings about everything.

Maybe this was a chance for things to go back to normal, to get back to my friends. That evening news gave me hope, but Monsieur told me the war was far from over. I liked that he knew so much about African politics. He used to tell me about the president of his home country, Laurent Gbagbo, and his policies. He despised government officials and corruption. To my teen ears, these were complicated subjects that I barely understood.

I sometimes complained about being away from Liberia, even during such tough times. I told Monsieur I didn't want to stay in America any longer as I was getting bullied at school. But Monsieur always knew how to make me see things differently. He wanted me to understand that America offered freedom unlike anywhere else. He told me America was only great at one thing and it was freedom — I did not have to fit in, because I could be anyone I wanted. We talked about the freedom to even get a new hair colour. He said I was in the freedom capital of the world. That was the most complicated thing I had read in our many months of emails. I thought about it the entire evening.

I went to school the following day excited to start exploring the idea of freedom in America. I wrote a draft of an email to Monsieur for my friends. I quickly caught them up on my life and my new school. I was having problems adjusting, but I didn't share that. I only talked about the free meals, students kissing in the hallways, the gothic kids, and other new things I saw around my school. My message to my friends was brief as I had to get back to my conversation with Monsieur. The cellphone bug had caught across Liberia, so I could reach some of my friends directly. By this time the war was over and things were slowly getting back to normal. But I wanted to hear more of Monsieur's ideas about creating my new identity. I wondered how he knew so much about America and her message of freedom.

That evening, I typed my email and hit send, waiting for his response. I waited until the next evening to check again. Nothing. Monsieur always answered my emails in less than a full day. This silence was new for him. *Perhaps Monsieur will reply in the morning,* I thought. He did not. I checked on my way to school and when I got back the next day. I repeated this for a week, and then another.

I finally asked my friend Zoe to check on Monsieur for me. She told me Monsieur had moved back to Ivory Coast in the middle of the night. He did not tell anyone. He just packed a few things and left. The landlord was still waiting to hear from him about what to do with his things in the apartment. I was devastated. I felt betrayed. We had shared so many secrets, and I thought he would at least tell me he was leaving. I kept writing to Monsieur in hopes of getting his personal email. He used his work email during our exchanges, so I had no way of hearing from him after he left Liberia. I don't know where Monsieur is or if he ever got his fantasy Liberian Wife after all.

The internet for me will always be a place where I could connect with my past while trying to create my new identity. It held my secrets and my teenage excitement, but mostly held me close to home. I think of Monsieur and the role he played in connecting me with my friends as the foundation for all my friendships on the internet throughout the years.

Many months later, I sent a message to the email I had used to connect with Monsieur:

Hello Monsieur,
Are you getting my messages? Please let me know
how I can contact you. Thanks.

The reply was instant:

Address not found
Your message wasn't delivered to the recipient
because the address could not be found, or is unable
to receive mail.

I COULDN'T HAVE BEEN THE ONLY ONE

Jon Sung

I just need to know if I was the luckiest idiot on the internet during the mid 00s or what. Stop me if you've heard this one before:

Sometime around 2002, I'd graduated college and had the great fortune to be both decent at my job and bored at work most of the time; I was also an avid reader of webcomics. One fateful day, one of my favourite comics announced it had started a message board. I signed up immediately. It turned out this board was part of a larger cluster of boards, many of which revolved around other comics I happened to read. One thing led to another, and . . .

Look, I'll just say it: the message boards I joined in the first half of the 00s were responsible for one hundred percent of the sex I had that decade.

None of us really ever talked about it back then and now I have questions: Was that a lot? Was everybody else on those boards also getting busy to the same degree? Was this happening on all the *other* message boards out there on the internet?

The first inkling we got that a whole other angle existed to all of our interactions that we hadn't even considered was probably the pictures. I have to imagine this was common across basically every message board community that existed: at some point, somebody was going to put up a picture that showed what they looked like. And then so would someone else. And then another. And so on. Attaching names to faces was always fascinating: Oh, that guy looks nothing like what I was imagining. Yikes, that other dude's hair is terrible. Wait, that user's a girl? So is that one? Huh: she's pretty. Oh no.

Oh *no*.

From such small files — laughably low-res JPEGs compared to the smartphone megapixel cornucopia we have access to in our pockets today, probably only 800 pixels wide, 1280 if you were feeling profligate with your bandwidth — were such crushes born. It was almost frighteningly easy, not just because you could see that a particular someone had a pretty face, but because the pictures inevitably captured something of their surroundings: you could see what this person's room looked like, what they hung on their wall, what colour their sheets were. It was like they'd transformed your computer momentarily into a magic window through which you could get a glimpse of what their life was like, and if you were lucky or smart or adept enough in some arcane art whose name you didn't even know, you could send yourself through that window to join them. In their room.

With those sheets.

You can see where I'm going with this.

That feeling on its own probably would've been enough, but then there were the boob threads. Did everyone else have those? It seemed like these were always started late at night, almost exclusively by female members who were feeling some combination of saucy and generous. WE'RE POSTING TOP- LESS PICS NOW IN HERE OKAY, THIS IS JUST WHAT WE'RE DOING. THANKS. Holy fucking shit, these threads. They didn't happen super often, but they happened enough, and when they did, all other activity on whatever board they were on seemed to grind to a halt. Of course, it's possible to infer and ascribe some less-charitable, attention-seeking motivations to them, but I swear at least some of that impulse came from a desire to reach out, to connect. Here, look at these: you like them? So do I. I've seen yours and I like those, too. These were notes played on the bass end of the scale, part of the rhythm section that you felt in your pants rather than your head, but they were still music, by god. And talk about a magic window: this wasn't just being granted a brief glimpse of that pretty person's room and imagining what it would be like to be there with them. You didn't even need to imagine! There were two utterly astounding things going on simultaneously: you could *literally see what they looked like naked,* and they were showing this to you freely. What a gift; what an insanely magnanimous, intoxicating gift.

Looking back, my two main reactions are (1) a distinct feel- ing that our message board culture still owes these pioneers a profound debt of thanks for busting us out of our collective shyness and (2) relief that none of us were fucking arrested.

I'm not saying anybody got laid as a direct result of the boob threads, but they were the most visible sign of the in-hindsight

obvious fact that we were — as the kids say — horny on main.
At least, they were the most visible sign on the actual message
boards, but there were the meetups, too. These were compar-
atively rare; most of us didn't make the kind of money that let
us fly all over the country at will. They usually happened in
conjunction with some kind of related event, like a comic convention, but sometimes, especially in the later years after we'd
been pals for a good long while, we'd just gather for the sake
of it. One of us would have an especially auspicious birthday,
or someone else might be moving out of their rented house
into someplace new and wanting to give their old place an
appropriate send-off.

Again I find myself wondering: surely other message boards
and their denizens had these, right? Did they also have the
same vibe? We were so excited to see each other, to be able
to exchange greetings and quips and jokes without having to
laboriously type them out. We could walk around as part of
one big knot of animated, almost manic people, so amped up
we were practically throwing off sparks.

Inevitably, as happens with meetups, you might find that one
of your crushes was also there. In person. You could see them
just as easily as you could see everyone else present, yes, but
suddenly the bandwidth of available information was exponen-
tially expanded: you could hear their voice along with everyone
else's as you walked to a restaurant, or see them smile in real-
time at some joke you made around a coffeeshop table. You
might find out what it felt like to hug them in enthusiastic greet-
ing. And somewhere in the back of your head, the knowledge
was clanging around that *they* could see *you,* too — that just as
you were drinking in everything about and around them, they

were at least theoretically able to do exactly the same thing back. What were they picking up? Did they . . . like what they were seeing? At night, when it was bunches of you standing around a house or a park with drinks in hand, and they sat down next to you, did that mean something? What was that smile about? Was this happening? No wonder we could barely sit still.

And so it would go: you'd be in a crowded motel room talking with a dozen others and they'd be parked on one of the beds with five other laughing people. And they might glance your way and scoot aside and smile as they patted the space next to them, and there it was: the tipping point where fevered supposition bloomed into sudden knowledge. (Of course, it might also be slightly more direct: you might be on your way into the bathroom and they might burst out of a stall, grab you by your lapels, and haul you back in for a frenzied makeout for which you were not at all prepared.)

That was how it happened: there'd be little clusters of us spread over a few houses or apartments or hotel rooms, and sometimes — maybe all the time — at least some of us, those lucky few (or not? was everybody doing this???) would find a private place to get it well and truly on. On other wholly separate occasions, some of us might find excuses and means to visit others in a faraway city for a more exclusive, one-on-one rendezvous.

Actually, that last part is conjecture; I'm extrapolating based on my own experience, which is to say I assume that since I sometimes did those things, surely others must have, too. But is that even true? I have no idea. I heard a rumour once — once! — about a couple at one of the communal meetups who fucked on a living room floor *in close proximity to others* who may or may not have been asleep at the time; the story wasn't very clearly told, and it somehow felt improper to pry. Was it true? Did it even happen?

Which is sort of the whole point of musing on this now: I have no idea if any of the sex I experienced was an outlier, or if it was just part of the usual fabric of message board life, or if I was actually on the *low* end of things sex-wise, and everybody else was secretly banging *way more than me.*

That last bit may be worth unpacking a little. On its face, it seems like a ridiculous conjecture, musings born from a kind of hand-wringing, furtive insecurity: "Is everybody else secretly having a way better time than me?" Because if I'm going to be honest with you, dear reader, I was kind of a late bloomer, and I knew it. Despite my best efforts, I didn't have a real girlfriend until my last year of high school. I was literally halfway through college before sex happened, and it took me by surprise in a set of circumstances that, looking back, seem like they would take some legitimate work for an outside observer to find credible. Whatever mojo I had didn't seem reliable in any way — I believed it was something outside of me, beyond my control: the capricious and unaccountable Sex Fairy would make an unseen visit to sprinkle me with Lucky Dust or she wouldn't, and in the meantime everybody else would be pairing up.

All of this is to say that now, in hindsight, it seems possible that I might've driven myself a little harder than average to seek out some lovin' in the post-college years when I was deep into the message board life; it's a short trip from "Is everybody else secretly having a way better time than me?" to "I bet they are," and from there to "Well, I've got some goddamn catching up to do!"

Intent alóne, however, does not a sex life make. That I experienced success in my endeavours was honestly kind of shocking. And here I have to wonder: Did the fact that we were all interacting on a message board make it easier to get it on? Did that teach me anything?

On some level, the answer has to be "maybe a little," right? You can read any number of poignant musings on how communicating in a primarily text-only, asynchronous medium like a message board makes it possible to tune your presence on said message board, to display only your best angles, your most refined and mirror-polished aspects, or even invent and present a wholly new and startlingly different persona. How much of me, or at least the me that everyone saw on my message boards, was an invention, a performance designed to dazzle and distract and entice?

As rhetorical as that question sounds, I think it's actually possible to answer in much more concrete terms: somewhere between one to ten percent, twenty-five percent at the most. Because look: there was nothing stopping you from puppeteering some kind of verbal impresario performance on the boards like a latter-day cyber Cyrano de Bergerac, but if you were truly making yourself a part of that board and the life thereon, you probably posted a picture or two of yourself at some point, and that meant someone — probably a lot of someones — knew what your sheets looked like. And once you'd been to a meetup or two, they knew what you sounded like when you talked and saw the face you made *that you couldn't even see*, the one you made when you weren't talking and were trying to think of the next thing to say. Once you were on the way to being alone in a room and naked with someone, your true self was going to show up eventually. You could pose for pictures and polish your prose to a mirror shine, but at some point your crush was going to find out what you smelled like, how you sounded when you laughed, what your whole-ass body looked like in a room with other people and clothes and books and things in it. Logic would seem to dictate that if message board-me had been one hundred percent a construct, then nobody would've stuck around once the artifice fell away and real-me made his debut. And I have to believe that a 50/50 mix of real-me/message board-me would still be a whiplash-inducing dealbreaker. So if we're going to accept that at least *some* of my message board presence was an act, it had to have been somewhere below fifty percent — probably quite a bit below. Maintaining a facade — even if it's just a facade on the internet constructed from words — takes *work,* and I know this about myself: I'm a profoundly lazy person. When it comes time to put fingers to keyboard, it's just easier to be myself than somebody or something else. So yes: message board-me was probably seventy-five to ninety-nine percent real-me.

So was it all good for me, in the end? Did I learn something? As I look back on that long-ago message board era now, I think I have learned something: It doesn't actually matter if anyone else from the boards was having more sex than I was, if I was just a denizen of merely average luck, or if I was somehow King of All Internet Sex-Havers without knowing it (which seems highly unlikely). All that's beside the point. Whatever sex I was having was helping me to accept myself, to finally acknowledge that what I was putting into the world had some effect on whether I could get laid; it wasn't all up to the whims of the Sex Fairy. Was I the luckiest idiot on the internet during the mid 00s? Yes and no, because it turns out the question voids itself in the asking. All that remains, the thing I'm still curious about, isn't even precisely whether everybody else on our message board and all the other message boards that existed was also getting super lucky, but rather, did they learn the same things I did, the same way?

My message board use tapered off as the decade wore on. By the time Tumblr came around, I hadn't been active on any of them for years — one of them had shut down long ago, in fact, a backend misconfiguration resulting in a cataclysm that triggered a diaspora of life-raft message boards that themselves eventually withered away. By then, I'd made friends I'd end up keeping for a lifetime, but never found The One, which meant I needed to find some other way to meet women. Where else was I to turn but the internet? So I learned how online dating — and as an inevitable consequence, real dating — worked. And I discovered something: somewhere in the tumult of message board life and meetups and sexual encounters great and small, I'd learned to be comfortable with myself around people I found attractive. As weird as it sounds, my online existence had taught me how to present myself in person: there was a lot about dating as a whole that I never liked, but I think I gave a much-better-than-average first date. My wife would probably agree: we met online, after all.

Yes, dear reader: I got married. That good first date led to several others, followed by moving in together and getting engaged. Our wedding seemed enormous, pushing past the two hundred mark, and could easily have been twice as big had budget and space not been concerns. The reason, funnily enough: the internet, specifically those early message boards.

My half of the guest list was at least one-third message board pals from that bygone era, culled with considerable effort from a much larger lineup. Many of us keep in touch to this day (Slack is a wonderful thing), talking about promotions at work, trading bread recipes, wrestling with politics and (lately) the joys and stresses of parenting — it's genuinely jarring to think about the sexy nonsense we got up to as a group a decade and a half ago. What would I tell my younger self, if I were able to step through a magical time portal and have a brief conversation at some late hour on a fervid online weeknight? Pay attention, I might say: it all works out in the end, but not exactly for the reasons you're thinking.

A LOVE LETTER TO THE BEAUTIFUL NAKED INTERNET GIRL OF 2003

Molly Crabapple

You had sardonic eyes beneath blunt-cut cyan bangs,
and they stared out at all of us like a dare.
You tattooed stocking seams up the backs of your
thighs. Tattoos, back then, were supposed to stand
in for rebellion.
You quoted — or misquoted — Georges Bataille.
You said you got into bar fights.
You posted photos of your torn-up knuckles to prove it.

In the year 2003, the internet was the perfect place for a
siren.

A girl, disconcerting, beautiful, bizarre, and above all unobtainable, singing a song that revealed exactly — and only — what
she wanted.

By the time I got acquainted with the sirens of the 2003 internet, I'd already been online for seven years. I got my social media start on Usenet. It was the right place for a precociously pretentious brat to escape the embarrassing travails of suburban middle school — a garden of words where I could attempt to write a new self into being, without needing the photos to back it up. Pretending to be older, I stalked groups for gothic fashion and radical politics, and fired off misspelled comments filled with the names of philosophers I had heard of but hadn't read. Thankfully, I used a fake name. I got into a few torrid email relationships with older men I never met, but a sense of dorky unreality hung over the whole business. A year later I got offline. Usenet couldn't compete with the trouble I made in real life, when I snuck into the city, shoplifted art books, and made out with artists whose names I didn't know in Central Park, then waited bleary eyed in the fluorescent-lit sprawl of Penn Station to catch the last creaking LIRR train home. *That* was adventure. Usenet was just a bunch of text.

I got online again at nineteen — as an art student who was trying her best to avoid honest employment, I was looking for ways to make cash, and the internet seemed like it could provide. It was 2002. At the time there was a small scene comprised of broke girls who were young, slim, and symmetrical enough to mimic hegemonic hotness in photos, and of men with a bit of cash and a professional camera who wanted these broke girls rolling around naked in their hotel rooms. The going rate was $100 an hour. Sometimes we were actually models, intent on being the fodder for artsy — or at least sexy — photos, but mostly we were serving the same function as private strippers, with the camera acting as a fig leaf. We found clients through sites like

OneModelPlace, a place where girls like me uploaded snapshots taken by our boyfriends, upon which we used our pirated copies of Photoshop to jack up the contrast (sophisticated!) and saturation (intense!). On our profiles we checked the boxes indicating our interests: Implied nude. TPF (trade for prints — meaning that we'd pose for free in exchange for professional photos). "Fashion" (ha!). Then we waited for the offers to roll in.

As I waited for the messages to pour in from potential clients, I scrolled through other models' profiles. Most were bog standard blondies, taut of body and mediocre of face, but some enthralled me. There was a Greek girl. Hair as black as an alcohol blackout. A generous mouth and half-closed eyes. A body perfectly curved, lush and innocent of exercise (anti-neoliberal, the Tumblr kids might say. It just was, without kale chips or SoulCycle. It didn't strive). I remember her posing in a crumbling hotel where you could rent rooms by the hour. Some ketamine-whacked artist had covered the walls with clown murals, but the room was spartan otherwise. The girl slouched against the in-room sink, her mascara smeared, her sloe eyes teary, her tank top hiked up over her pointed olive breasts. Neither the photographer's fisheye lens nor his sadistic angles could efface a beauty as fine as hers. But it wasn't just the Greek girl's physical presence that slayed me — it was the life implied by her photos. She was in LA one day, London the next, transforming herself for each shoot until her portfolio resembled a card deck of clichéd but glamorous femme archetypes: angel, fan dancer, nymph. Her life reminded me of the biographies I loved of 19th century courtesans; they too were working-class, self-constructed women who created independent futures by turning each of their gestures into art.

> I followed your name online through the wormhole
> that is Google, looking for traces of you that I could
> worship or envy. I wanted to bang you. I wanted to be
> you. I watched you on forum posts, in DIY porn sets,
> thinking of how I might ever approach your self-pos-
> session, your slender thighs, your fuck-off style.

Later that year, a photographer friend shot me for a tattooed naked girl website whose fame has faded but whose litigious nature remains. HomicideBabes, let's call it. HB took the standard porn site fare — sets of fifty photos in which the girl gets increasingly naked with each shot — but added to this the pretence of feminist badassery. We were encouraged to show our personalities in our sets. At various times, HB models wielded broadswords, pretended to snort diamonds, and dressed up like Baby Jane. We were also encouraged to maintain blogs on the site and post on its forums. Management touted this as further proof of their feminism — we HomicideBabes weren't silent dollies, but fully rounded humans, as confessional or as bitchy as we pleased. With one exception, spelled out on the Models FAQ: "Please don't mention your significant other. We like to preserve a sense of mystery."

Nonetheless, we were several hundred internet naked girls, insubordinate, clever, and mouthy, our vanity swollen by the thousands of worshipful comments posted on the message boards beneath our pictures, then dashed if the HB management refused to buy more of our photos. Ostensibly equal, the site had stars, and I spent days online staring at these queens. The six-foot-tall Latvian model with the razor cheekbones, who overpainted her lips like a drag queen and posed with a luchador mask and a glitter-encrusted strap-on. The tanned LA ice queen, her body a gallery of intricate tattoos, whose left leg was severed just above the knee. The boyish blonde in roller skates who quoted Foucault. Later they would be replaced with the very young, silent, and skinny girls favoured by the site's male owner, but for now they were all there, swaggering, preening, offering admonishments then solidarity, but never ever getting paid what they were worth.

I would never be one of these girls. I weighed too much. I was too awkward. I had zero ability to charm the site's management. I never learned how to do my eyebrows, nor to properly blow out my hair. Some nights I would pick apart their pictures and blog posts, trying to deduce the essence of what made them stars and wondering if I could obtain it.

> You were slim as a young cat, smirking and tetchy, swollen-eyed, swollen-mouthed, utterly intimidating in your men's underwear and your stained old t-shirt for a band whose drummer you had banged but whose name I was not cool enough to know, relaxing before your spot at a painfully corporate burlesque show. You sucked a cigarette. You did not want to be disturbed backstage.

Though we were naked online, we had a privacy that seems unobtainable for internet girls of this age, naked or otherwise. No one knew our real names. Despite occasional "drama" over who copied whose tattoos, we seldom seriously fought. And while we were hypnotised by the torrent of flattery our photos elicited, the site was not designed to be a virtual B.F.

Skinner box the way that Twitter and Facebook are now. HomicideBabes did not feed us constant mini hits of dopamine
and outrage, just as it did not bring about Reality Show US
Presidents, Kiddie Concentration Camps, Black Pill Mass
Shooters, or Threats of Nuclear War. Most of all, in this time
before smartphones, we left our lives at HomicideBabes on
the desktop computer. Only rarely did a fan approach me
in public. The internet had not yet bled completely into the
physical world.

We did not yet have the influencer economy. Traditional
jobs (media or otherwise) had not yet disappeared, and asking
for money online still had a disreputable air. The only people
who solicited donations or hawked their Amazon wishlists
were internet harlots like us. Later, more respectable sites stole
our techniques. What is Patreon after all but the interface
for a single girl pay site — the dollops of content for steady
support — but now used by lefty podcasts and fascist You-
Tubers. (Ironically, adult content is ghettoised on Patreon
and does not turn up on search results. Internet naked girls, so
useful in a site's early days, are shunted off when it starts to go
mainstream. A digital gentrification not unlike the "cleaning
up" of Times Square.) As HomicideBabes, we posed for a
corporate site, sometimes in panties emblazoned with their
corporate logo, but most of us had little conception of a capitalism that was bigger than a neighbourhood head shop. Instead,
we had constant hustles — gogo gigs, selling our panties on
Craigslist — while the boss accumulated the real cash from
our images. But while we were at his whims, we did not need
to optimise ourselves for the great algorithmic maw, compiled
from the whims of everyone.

You wrote long, searching LiveJournal entries about your hick town, about Hunter S. Thompson, about addiction, about hopping boxcars and falling in love with the sky.

You mashed your tits together for the camera, gave a campy pout, and then burst out laughing at everyone who had been enough of a sucker to buy a subscription to your pay site.

When I was pregnant, you gave me frank advice about what sort of abortion I should get.

You disappeared somewhere, to grow weed, go to medical school, get married, make babies, become normal, or become a star.

You were many girls, and no girl, and every girl, because in the content soup that pours through our devices, our images become one image comprised of ones and zeroes.

Perhaps I was once you in another woman's eyes.

In 2019 the beautiful internet naked girls are made of savvier stuff than I was in 2003. Unlike me, they don't need to depend on guys with cameras to take their photos. They have self-facing phone cameras, tripods, and timers. They own the means of production and can churn their own images for a whole panoply of platforms. They have Venmos and Instagrams and wishlists and Snapchats and Clips4sale. The forced transparency of the internet has made real something feinted at by Homicide-Babes — the naked girl as a fully rounded human being. I often see the same babe post two videos on one Twitter account. In the first, she's twerking in a thong. In the second, she's starring in a slickly self-produced video, giving commentary on *Caliban and the Witch*. And while the digital space for sex workers has brutally shrunk, thanks to SESTA and FOSTA, there is a sex workers' rights movement far more diverse, developed, and relentless than anything I would have recognised at nineteen. They intimidate me, these girls. They're too optimised, their branding too on point, the personal information they share too cautious. The internet, after all, is a place less wild and less friendly than it was. As everyone got online, there's less space to play, to try, or merely to be. Everyone is hustling, grasping, and fighting. Rest is an illusion — something you post pictures of to build your brand.

I am thirty-six, and my days as a professional naked girl have receded far enough into the past to be just a fillip on my biography. My former naked girl friends have fought their ways to positions of power. But on an internet that seemed safer despite all the old people who warned us endlessly of its danger, I still remember what we once were.

> I miss your gothy pseudonyms, the wild experimen-
> tation, the embrace of decadence.
> I miss you, beautiful naked girl of 2003.
> Siren, crush, friend, comrade.

RELEASE THE STARS

Melissa Gira Grant

Sometime in the 1990s, before anything had happened, the new owners of the bar that would become the Lone Palm planted one just outside its door. A queen palm. A claim-staking. I was leaning into his arm, crossing Guerrero going west on 22nd Street just after sunset, the first time I saw it.

Friday, June 22, 2007. He was a brace against the broken asphalt, dressed in collared shirt and tie and high-waisted trousers, and I wore a dress that fell just at knee-length, high heels with an open toe and straps across the ankles. It would have been getting cold. I felt his warmth, passing under the soft neon glow over the door, the black-and-white film rolling in an aging VHS at the far end of the bar. It smelled like rose water.

Inside, we took a two-top, with a white tablecloth and a votive in glass in the middle. After he pulled my chair out for me and I placed my purse at my side and he was seated, we were two of the only people to lay our phones beside the candles, both Nokias. We had been sending each other photos all day. He was the first person to do that, with me. They looked like the film. So did his hair, slicked high-contrast back from his forehead, dyed darker than natural, I thought, and with one thin bleached streak. This was just the second time I had seen him in person since we met — and we had met in person, too, in Los Angeles, not on the internet. At the American Film Institute, there was a weekend festival to introduce creators of online video two years on from the launch of YouTube. Unlike most people I met for the first time there, I did not know him online at all.

Maybe that's because that was his job. The company's foray into online video was like that of an already elder generation. I was seventeen the summer the company that employed him went public, and that was in 1995. That was just before the palm was put in the ground, before we got here, too. In our own way, we were running out of time: just about and just over thirty between us, and we had missed the big old days, the "crazy" years, when the neighborhood around us flooded with previously unimagined cash and the young white people who had been paid it. Of course, no one was wealthy, the legend passed down went. It was just on paper. So many of their companies disappeared with their projected net worth, and that was that. When we moved here, a few years later, it was quiet. No one felt they had to found anything of world-changing importance, and the bars were emptier.

San Francisco. There were palms all over this neighborhood, huge ones in the park spanning two big blocks of rolling green off the west side of the Mission Dolores, from which the neighborhood took its name. The Mission (the neighborhood) was a survivor, too: a lone fire hydrant is credited with saving its wooden houses and the Mission Dolores itself from the fires a century before, the great earthquake, and in tribute, it's now painted gold. In a place where the story of itself is told as if it started just one generation before that catastrophe, the few years dividing us from the last bust made that event already historic, too. If you stayed in the city after the dot-com crash, then you were faithful. If you moved there after, you were devoted. You still believed in San Francisco, and also the thing that nearly tore San Francisco apart.

History is what drew us together in a theatre in Los Angeles, or old things, anyway. Before the screenings started that day, I had seen him carrying a caramel-brown leather suitcase from the 1940s, and he noticed the vintage cream silk scarf I had tied at my neck. To the festival organizers, it felt important to put internet videos on the big screen, to lend them its anachronistic significance. And why else were we wearing and carrying these things ourselves? The Sunday morning program we both chose and sat beside each other for was curated around sex. As the lights came up again, I left with his name and Flickr username on a piece of paper. I said I was a writer and I ran a blog about sex and the internet. He said he was kind of fucked up about his job because he ended up looking at a lot of porn.

He was a content moderator, essentially. His job at the old internet company was a mirror to the festival: to program videos for the site's various landing pages, featuring those he thought would attract an audience back to the website and flagging those that the company might not want to have featured.

But he was also a photographer and a visual artist. The website, he thought, could be a platform for similar creators to share their work and meet one another. (A forever festival, or maybe the festival was a two-day website.) He was also a particular kind of fetishist, so he would linger over those videos just shy of violating the company's terms of service. An electric blue pump sliding into the mud. Honey drizzled over a woman's leg in a black nylon stocking. A man in a full latex bodysuit, slipping and falling, then trudging forward to turn off the camera.

Most of these videos were only as long as a "view" made and projected on the Lumière Brothers' *Cinématographe* from the 1890s — a snippet, not a story. The old internet company's homepage was even at times styled to look like an early 20th century traveling movie road show, a striped tent with a screen and *SECRETS!* inside and nothing more than cloth and a barker standing between the general public and the sights to be seen beyond. The man at the door was both promoter and protector.

His job was to watch these and decide which to suppress from view on landing pages, which to remove. He sent me the links before deleting them. He asked, "Is this pornography?"

//

The subject line of his first message to me was automated, and it was:

[Flickr] You are [— —]'s newest contact!

A second message followed:

> I'm so glad we met. We must needs [sic] have
> a pornographic meeting of minds (meeting
> of pornographic minds or whichever).

(I break in here to say, now, then, I love this doubling.)

> Maybe we can figure out how to write it
> individually/jointly.

I replied:

> I'm all for this meeting of the minds to con
> tinue. Clearly we have more conspiring to do.

(I break in again, to note: I chose not to edit out the clichéd word "conspiring" after the fact, because it sets up something that follows.)

> Can I make the not at all bold suggestion of
> coffee (or a cocktail) sometime this week?
> Let's see what we can find between our
> two heads and histories.

He replied, changing the subject to "Conspirators of Pleasure," the title of a 1996 film by Jan Švankmajer, and which the director described at the Prague premiere as "the first erotic film in which there is no sexual intercourse."
He wrote:

> Where pornography is concerned, it's never
> the minds that meet. But I'm all for subverting
> the expected anatomical order of things.
> My preference is almost always for the coc
> tail. I simply like them better.

> I'd love to do it this week, but I'll have to
> let you know. My wife returns from Germany
> today and so my social calendar is up in the
> air for the moment. But yes, soon.
> This week if possible.
> I'm really excited about this prospect. Let's
> take over the world.

Some time after receiving the message, I wrote, and only to myself:

His first email… I got it while exiting the bus in front of my apartment on Sutter Street so I may not have been thinking straight when I came to the words "my wife"… I paused at the sign there on the side of the road that just said "California Parking" crested by palm trees, the only hint we were somewhere people thought it looked like. I thumbed back up to the top of his email on my phone. "Sunday at the Orbit Room sounds just right."

But I did not write that email, not in those words. I wrote and I sent something else from my phone, standing on the street as I remembered even as I lost the words, and on what was the Sunday after the one on which we had met, I arrived — knowing about the wife, with or without my scarf at my neck, and in black kidskin heels, phone in my hands, and offering my hands on the bar made of copper and zinc.

"The tense, symbolic quality of the gesture — hands, legs, ears — for some reason the lips on the ear, we're always in a whispered engagement," I wrote to myself, after that evening, and after we had been talking about the French literary critic and philosopher Roland Barthes, "leaning in, bending, also the cupping of the back of the neck in the palm, fingers curled slightly, maybe into the hair. My own navigates automatically now there, to tug and stroke the hair at the back of my neck, as he did. Our sign, for the imminent kiss. Also, absence, but." ("To speak amorously is to expend without an end in sight," wrote Barthes, "without a *crisis*; it is to practice a relation without orgasm.")

He worked all day, and theoretically, so did I. The blogging wasn't really a job, but I had decided to treat it as one anyway. Our chat windows were open throughout, and in certain stolen moments — company time, his and mine — a photograph would arrive on my phone. That night, a variation of it might appear on his Flickr.

I started making short, silent clips. The silver sun through fog and half-closed blinds, coming into my studio apartment. The choppy light on my face through the streetcar window, rumbling down Market towards the Castro. A from-above shot of my leg under a wrought-iron table, giving it the shadow of fishnets. It didn't matter what we shot, just that we could do it so easily and that we could show one another, quickly. The working definition of online microcelebrity was just the desire to be famous to fifteen people at a time. Posting these only confirmed: *you all can see this is happening.* So I wore heels everywhere. I carried a digital camera that could shoot fine video and fit in a 1940s handbag without bowing it at the edges. I played the same Rufus Wainwright album all the time. "Didn't you know that old Hollywood is over?"

The movies still played at the Lone Palm, where he wore a wedding ring and remarked (though he disputed this later) that Friday nights were usually reserved for "his wife." Now we had exchanged dozens of photos, hundreds of texts, and seen one another exactly three times, only ever in public. His next proposal was that we produce a video series together. We could use my studio — my studio apartment down the hill from Grace Cathedral. We were already asking ourselves, would it ruin this if it went much further?

//

He put me in a taxi home, back to lower Nob Hill, from the Lone Palm. He got home to the email from me already: a link to a secret blog I had registered for us, for the show. We would start the following weekend. *The show* is what he would tell his wife, as he packed two of her cocktail glasses, his cufflinks, and a fresh white shirt in the caramel-brown suitcase.

Me, I owed no one anything. *The show* was clearing room in the small sitting room space across from my bed so we could put up lights. *The show* was traipsing in heels up Nob Hill a few blocks to buy a cocktail shaker someone was selling from a blanket spread on the sidewalk. I didn't have the money he did. I didn't have a wife to tidy for me.

There was one way I had money, but it was unpredictable — a friend of a friend would be coming into town, someone connected to the business that used to be done in the private message sections of online escort boards. We would shoot on Sunday, a month to the day from the day we met, and on Friday I would go to the East Bay to make my rent.

We talked all day now, chat to phone to chat and back.

Sometimes, he wouldn't offer any commentary, just paste the URL into the text box for me to offer my own determination. "Parody or porn?"

Me: "Parody." Meaning it could stay. "And so far they haven't made a single 2257-breach."

He sent another. "I labeled this one 'crushing videos for the Pop art set.' She should have crushed a Brillo box."

Me: "Or a mylar pillow."

Him: "Is this stuff worth adding to our blog?"

Me: "This could be a segment on our show."

The day before, I went to refresh my hair. For the show, for the work. We chatted while I was in the chair, in front of the mirror — I took my laptop everywhere, and the salon had wifi. He had just gotten his trim, he said, and took the chance to tell his hairdresser about me, the show, Los Angeles. "He would love you."

Me: "He may already."

Him: "Possibly."

"I'm being called away."

"Go then."

"Bye until blonde."

June 29, 2007. I woke up in the studio becoming a studio. Except for tea, there was nothing in the kitchen. My cream scarf was hung on a scavenged statue of David in my entryway, near the alcove where the telephone once would have been. Would he remember it? I didn't feel like seeing this client, so I imagined I was dressing instead for him: a midi-length dress in a tawny taupe from one of the big box stores lining the streets from the transbay train to my apartment. (I emailed him beforehand: "Buy the dress, commit the crime," after a photo I found far back in his Flickr, and which I asked him about that morning, which he had captioned, "He remembered saying, as the picture snapped: 'This is the picture right before the crime.'" Under that, I put on seamless taupe nylon stockings that cost at least twice what the dress did and weren't made anymore. *Everything I love about you is old.* My phone charged, I left.

From Sutter Street, I turned down Stockton, and I could see them, lining the sidewalks around the Apple Store on Post Street. It was early, but warming up fast enough that I didn't need my sweater. But these people looked like they had been camped here all night. I held my Nokia in my hand as I walked past quickly, not taking any pictures, careful not to trip on their camp chairs. At the corner I came to them: two carnival barkers, garish and pastel, San Francisco's own clowns in a gutter bordered by glass. They were promoting nothing at all, their commentary to this other spectacle, the first iPhone Day line.

Hours later, he was off work and I was back at Market and Montgomery, richer and walking into the Palace Hotel bar, taking two seats before the painting by Maxfield Parrish that stretched its whole length. Another earthquake survivor, the hotel was now the city's oldest still standing, even if the original had to be torn down and a new one built in its place. The painting arrived then. It was the story of the Pied Piper.

He had a gift: *The Philosophy of Andy Warhol*. (I turned the page down at this part: "Sex is a nostalgia for sex.") Over three martinis each, we outlined the show. Later, I placed the notes from our conversation that evening onto our days-old secret blog:

cuckolding — for the future

etymology, the porn sense of the word,

sex and THE SPECTACLE

...

not just gratuitous, to set the stage, but to seduce

the viewer

'suffer the naked leg'

the dialectic

...

seducing the viewer

we can't give them everything they want

what is it to share a touch that no one else ought to

know about?

'do they or don't they?'

...

how do we shoot this?

how do we talk about porn again?

PORN is the very intersection of sex.

i am sick of pornography

porn is the easiest way to access this thing called

sex

(The morning I began work on this part of the story, I texted him and asked by way of what I called fact-checking which Roland Barthes — *A Lover's Discourse* or *Pleasure of the Text* — it was he left in my apartment, and he replied, "Oh. I've been wondering where that went. I think I may have your 'text.'"

As Barthes wrote in the one that he did leave in my apartment, "He who utters this discourse and shapes its episodes does not know that a book is to be made of them; he does not yet know that as a good cultural subject he should neither repeat nor contradict himself, nor take the whole for the part; all he knows is that what passes through his mind at a certain moment is *marked*, like the printout of a code."

Soon after he asked, "Are you fact-checking for your memory or your memoir?")

I sent him off from the Palace — Friday, the night with the wife — and texted the person I actually was having sex with. Climbing the hill again, there was no trace of the scene outside the Apple Store. I threw my hand open-palmed out to brace myself against a building abutting it, rounding the corner: I could not see. The drinks in the dark had dropped a filter over the neighborhood. But the sun was still out. Somehow I got into my apartment and onto the bed, in my heels and stockings and dress and all, and saw the person was on his way. I would pass out then and wake up only once the person was downstairs.

Fixing myself, I saw I had typed a text about the book to him and had not sent it.

Too wasted for sex, the person took me to a party instead, in the part of the city where warehouses had long been converted or torn down for condos. Outside, avoiding most of it, three people were standing around this thing otherwise in the dark. They weren't friends but I knew them from Twitter, so I knew before seeing it was an iPhone. One of them handed it to me. We watched a video. It was just so smooth to touch.

//

The conceit was that of an old radio show, where the voices traveled into your home perhaps uninvited, but with moving pictures and about the present-day. A video blog with an audience of two.

Him, the morning after: "I was just watching the feed from your camera."

Me: "Oh?"

"Clearly we had a good time. I think though, we could come up with a more advantageous angle for you. It's just all shoulder and hair. And occasionally my hand."

"Mmm, no, I need a tripod."

"We need your eyes."

Me: "Or, the reverse POV shot, like how 'your camera' was really mine."

Pause.

Me: "Yes, eyes and my cupid's bow. It does all the work for me."

Him: "You have a lovely mouth."

Pause.

Him: "It's not just delusion? We're good?"

Me: "We are. As many difficulties as we had with tech, not having the strictest script ... "

Him: "And that's not just a ruse to get me drunk in your bed again?"

Me: "I'll tell you when I get to the rest of the audio on my train ride."

Later, him: "I'll just say stuff to our blog. It's odd, a little self-reflexively voyeuristic to listen to our show."

Me: "I love this thought, of speaking to the blog. Our chaperone."

//

I thought the palm had always been there. I didn't know it was planted in 1991, just before the bar had a name. Only later its pink neon Art Deco sign set the leaves aglow. They went in that order: signal, and then scene. They had to put the palm in for anything there to happen.

"What will she think?" I asked him, after we had logged nearly six hours of tape, but hadn't published anything. His wife, I emphasised, was also on the internet. She had just excused herself from the table. By then she insisted on spending time with me, too. He and I would go off on our own after brunch, pretend it was just drinking or the cold (it was July) that made us put our hands on each other.

"She'll understand," he said in a breezy way, just the two of us before she returned to her seat. "She's in the theatre."

STAYING VIGIL

Catherine Tan

The covenant of blood is thicker than the water of the womb, as the saying goes. The modern equivalent "blood is thicker than water" is used somewhat inaccurately to underscore the importance of family. However, the original saying was an homage to kinship and loyalty, to the strength of bonds forged in moments of crisis and fear.

I'm twenty-seven and I sit awake, watching Notre Dame burn. It is the middle of the night and all is silent except for the singing of hymns by devastated Parisians. There is a sense of bleakness as the spire falls. My mind recalls other instances of similar pain and hopelessness. Grenfell Towers. Storms devastating regions like Puerto Rico, Haiti, New Orleans, Aceh. Terrorist attacks in Mumbai, London, Paris —

The night my father died.

Nineteen-year-old me sits awake in front of a computer. I can't remember when I last slept. Certainly not that night, but maybe the night before. All my tears have gone and I am in a chatroom. My siblings in all but blood are there with me, taking time out of their day in a show of kinship and loyalty that I had never experienced before, nor since.

//

It is 2005. The heat in the classroom is oppressive, the teacher's voice an incessant drone. Outside, cicadas shriek, and with my head propped on my fist, I dream.

Like many fourteen-year-olds, my focus isn't on a distant future, but just an hour or two later. When the last bell rings, I will pack my bag and head home. In the living room, my computer sits ready. My bag will thump on the floor, and with the press of a button, my computer will turn on.

I struggle to communicate the state of isolation that I existed in during this time. It wasn't something I was actively aware of. A deep-sea fish born to absolute darkness never misses the light or the warmth of the sun. The bright colours of the coral reef and its inhabitants are a universe away. From the earliest days of primary school, I watched shoals of classmates as they interacted, constantly trying to understand what it was that made friendships work. A recent reunion with those same classmates indicated that they had no idea I was suffering that much socially. I suspect that a developmental disorder is at the root of this, and my teacher (who I was close to in those years) agreed.

Attempting to make friends was an exercise in tenacity. I would simply attach myself to a group and hope that my presence would stick. I had nothing in common with my classmates and had no idea how to make small talk. Instead of seeming interested, I tried to seem interesting. Given the plutonian slant of my character (I was always deeply interested in death, spirituality, mythology, and folklore), talking about my interests brought me mixed success at best. At worst, it seemed to strike fear into those around me. The children I knew at that time were more interested in the TV shows that were popular, such as in *Pokémon*, *Digimon*, *Cardcaptor Sakura*, and *Sailor Moon*. All these shows were not amongst the media I consumed; I grew up watching documentaries. Whilst various fads in childhood games came and went, I collected the accoutrements, such as Pokémon cards or the neon-coloured plastic pieces that were part of a local game called *kuti kuti*. However, none of these props served to help me mask my social deficits or ease my sense of loneliness.

Fortunately, my foray into digital friendships proved to be an easier journey.

In 2005, smartphones did not exist. There were a variety of mobile phones — from the bar-shaped offerings of Nokia to the slide phones by Sony Ericsson, and Samsung represented Asia with flip phones — however, access to the internet from these devices was still iffy, slow, and expensive.

Because the internet could not yet be carried with you and was intrinsically reliant on a computer and broadband connection, it became a distinct and separate realm of its own. Sitting alone in the living room, I felt like a scuba diver or the pilot of a deep-sea vessel. Or perhaps I was a cosmonaut, exploring alien landscapes, completely distant and separate to the realities of my life.

On the internet there was a distinct sense of freedom — and of possibility. It was the time of Web 2.0, where Twitter hadn't yet launched and YouTube was barely four months old, and there was a clear division between real life and online life. This division fueled the imagination, allowing the user to be as creative or as honest as they wished to be. There was a certainty in the right to privacy and anonymity.

In those days I sometimes dreamt of a complete integration of real life and the internet. A world where the internet was ever present, readily accessible. I wanted a world in which my online friendships were not just contained in screens, a world where games were a part of real life, where people in my offline world, my *real world*, could see that I too had friends and people who valued me. When I was fourteen, I dreamed of the 2010s, imagining an overlay of digital and real worlds, not realising the implications.

//

It is late in the afternoon on September 6, 2005. I scroll through the list of active chatrooms on DeviantArt. DeviantArt functioned as a precursor to most portfolio sites on the internet today; it served as a space for artists to connect, to share their content, and to get and give critique. It catered to both amateurs and professionals, and even allowed one to define their stage of learning and their preferred artform. At that point, like many teenagers on the internet in the early 2000s, I am in the midst of an anime phase, and join DeviantArt to follow my favourite artists and learn from the tutorials that the website served as a repository for. Most chatrooms on the site are targeted towards a specific artform, like photography, writing, or digital painting. But all I intend to do is while the hours away, not embark upon technical discussions with people much older than myself. Eventually, I find a chatroom more my speed: DAUnderworld, a chatroom themed after the *Underworld* movie. My alias is ice_evanesco, using a spell from *Harry Potter and the Order of the Phoenix*.

Despite the odd hour, conversation is lively. I introduce myself and settle in to watch. The chatroom is a mix of roleplay and discussion, a style distinctive to the chatroom and community here.

A heated debate starts to escalate. All other conversation ceases. Suddenly I find myself in a tavern where a bar brawl seems about to erupt, and that is *exactly* what happens. People start laying bets on the combatants. One member collates the betting pool. I contemplate the viability of hiding under an imaginary table or chair. Over the years I had grown used to being a bystander, accepting the isolation that came with my idiosyncratic personality. That day, I throw caution to the wind. I am sick of being a bystander, and it's a low-risk opportunity to get involved in a community. If they don't like me, I can just move on. I seize the chance to set up a stall between the onlookers and brawlers, dispensing weapons to further fuel the combat. It seemed like a logical choice at that point in time, a way to participate without being intrusive.

My willingness to participate in ongoing shenanigans endears me to the chatroom and I am welcomed into the fold. We spend nights and days in that chatroom, using the anonymity of usernames to discuss everything that matters and some things that do not. Our usernames become our alter-egos, allowing us to create the people we want to be.

Ironically, who we most wanted to be were *ourselves*. We wanted to be able to express who we believed we truly were — the thoughts and feelings that we were learning to keep repressed, the words we wanted to share that were too controversial for public consumption. We wanted to be the people that we could be without the strictures of society, the expectations of family, and the pressures of daily life. Sometimes we talked about our futures, where we wanted to go, how we wanted to live. A chatroom where we didn't have to show our faces became the perfect canvas for us; with bold ideas as brush strokes and our hopes as paint, we drew our self-portraits. Each username became more than just a label for a nameless and faceless individual. We became more than our physical appearances or social statuses, more than stereotypes of "outsider" and "that weird one." I loved being able to bypass all meaningless social convention like small talk to directly peer into another creative's heart, the crucible of their soul.

Being a few years older than myself, my friends guided me through the difficulties of teenage life. As a relatively sheltered Asian teenager, I only had two major spheres of life to contend with: school and family. My troubles primarily revolved around school. I did relatively well in academics but struggled to make and maintain friendships. Some days felt more difficult than others, as certain stimuli would set me off. It could be the pervasive heat of the tropics, the noise of a class of restless teenagers, or even the constant and overwhelming presence of a friend. To the outside world, I probably seemed like a moody, irascible, and unpredictable teenager, and not knowing any better, I thought that this was all par for the course, a part of growing up.

At home, I was the eldest child to strict Asian parents. Like many parents exposed to the new challenge of their children being on the internet, mine are initially concerned about me being hoodwinked or catfished. My father is especially disapproving of my chatroom friends. At times, he tries to ban me from the computer. Other times, he threatens to smash it. He installs parental control software; I find my way around it. We were fighting an age-old battle, a parent's concern pitted against a teenager's need for freedom. The arena, however, was different.

I learn subterfuge, to come home early and use the computer in the afternoon hours before my father gets home. He says hurtful things about my friends. I occasionally argue back, prompting shouting matches. *If he could see them, if he could meet them, he would understand,* I think, wanting more than ever for technology to catch up, to make the virtual *real*. My chatroom friends explain how his concerns are legitimate, subtly prodding at me to learn to step out of my shoes and to develop my cognitive empathy.

//

It is 2006 and my father has just been diagnosed with leukemia. Home life changes drastically. My mother divides her time between the hospital, home, and work. Being the eldest daughter, it suddenly falls upon me to take care of my younger siblings. I am fifteen, and they are twelve and eight.

My father's hospital ward becomes our second home, and the nurses are kind to us. We learn that the cheapest drinks can be bought from the vending machines a floor down, outside the pediatric wards. I push my youngest sister on the swings in the playground outside.

Sometimes we spot a pale face peeking at us from the wards. We feel guilty, for apparently revelling in the face of suffering. We want to make friends — but wary of encroaching, we pretend nothing else exists. The sun shines upon us, as the pale, sickly faces of children made sheet-white by harsh artificial lights look on.

The pressure of work had turned my father ill-tempered over the years. Upon his diagnosis, his doctor advises him to relax and take things positively. Cancer is as much a mental game as it is a physical ailment, he explains. My father complies, and over time, he becomes calm, patient, and jovial. The time he spends at home is spent on us. He cooks, we talk and watch shows together, and he catches up on missed time.

Like the hospital playground, our home life becomes a bubble, protecting us from confronting sickness and the quiet pacing of time. For my fifteenth birthday, my father buys me a guitar. We keep delaying having him teach me. The guitar still sits, unused.

Surprisingly, he also starts to spend time on the computer. Cooped up at home, he starts to use the internet to alleviate his boredom and need for social interaction. My father and I develop a strange bonding ritual; with the two desktops side by side, we sit in mutual silence, talking to people online. As a bird-keeping hobbyist, he becomes somewhat of an expert on pet forums, teaching others the ins and outs of choosing and rearing songbirds. I laugh at my screen and tell my dad about DAUnderworld shenanigans. Over time, he grows to accept the people there as individuals, and as my friends. My mom leaves us to it. Unlike us, she has never been a night owl.

//

The bone marrow transplant is successful. Now in remission, my father goes back to work in late 2007. Precautions are set up by his employer. My father is to work in an isolation room, to prevent infection. All it takes is for one visitor to ignore the sign. One sneeze.

My father ends up in the intensive care unit on a respirator. It is January 2008; he has a triple infection of his lungs. I am sixteen and watching my father fight for his life.

I start sleeping less and less, waiting every night for a phone call from the hospital. My father doesn't sleep at all. He is on sedation, but somehow fights the drugs with sheer willpower.

Despite everything, he is discharged to spend the Chinese New Year at home. On February 7, 2008, on the first day of the Lunar New Year, his lung collapses. Ambulances are called.

He has the upper lobe of his right lung removed. I start at a new school the next week. It is what my father wants. He wants me to do the A-levels and go to university.

Whilst my father is in hospital, and my mother is by his side, I try to do my best to ease their worries, caring for my sisters and catching up on my schoolwork. I have neither the energy nor emotional capacity to attempt to get to know my classmates at this new school. As my real life becomes rapidly destabilised, DAUnderworld becomes my primary support system, and the older members become my surrogate siblings.

> 16:14:36 * ice-evanesco has been sitting in front of
> the computer the whole day, and hasn't done most
> of the work assigned
> 16:15:05 <onefourth> ice-evanesco: :(
> 16:16:00 <ice-evanesco> onefourth: it's not my
> fault. okay, it's my fault. but don't kick me out to

make me do my work.
16:16:15 <onefourth> ice-evanesco: Go do
your work.
16:16:22 <onefourth> or i shall shun you
16:16:55 <ice-evanesco> onefourth: please don't!
16:17:11 * ice-evanesco is busy: doing work now

Members like onefourth, Sorrowburn, Deadrosebud, Anfalas, and Alisette encourage me in their own ways. SorrowBurn in my mind is a grumpy Viking. An avid reconstructionist, his city is often treated to the sight of him smuggling swords wrapped in trash liners. When it floods we tell him to get the longboat out to paddle down to the shop. At some point he did some work with mental health, and he somehow keeps my mental health from fraying too badly.

Deadrosebud is a vintage-loving academic. Her altar is dedicated to Aphrodite, festooned in pearls and a beautiful statuette. She is also an archer. She is as smart as she is beautiful, as dangerous as she is smart. Like a cat, the essence of her cannot be measured by vessel or scale.

Anfalas has the personality of a sun god who forgets he has incarnated into a human form. He admits to having a large ego, but the verdict is out on whether his heart is larger still. He jokes with me and keeps me laughing. In the entire four years of struggle with my father's illness, that laughter is precious.

Pyronixcore is sometimes aloof, but he is caring and warm-hearted. He is deeply self-reflective, an ocean of churning thought. As a member of the LGBTQ+ community, he inspired me to become an ally in a time when such issues were taboo.

Darkrosefairy77 is a fae soul, drawn to both nature and all things sparkly. Smart and streetwise, she exudes maturity despite being younger than me. Her daring nature reminds me constantly of the very spirit of impetuous youth, what it is like to be courageously weird, gloriously strange.

Alisette is my study buddy during this time. We both want to go to university and encourage each other. We commiserate in the student struggle and the anxiety of potentially graduating into an uncertain economic climate. Sometimes we discuss writing and our creative pursuits. Other times, she helps me think rationally, discern reality from my disordered thought patterns.

By now, we know each other better than I could ever know any of my friends in real life. Perhaps it's my fault. I endeavour to keep home and school separate, in a bid to protect myself. I have no desire to have my classmates pity me. As broken down as I am becoming, I am still a prideful creature. I feel a deep, irrational need to appear competent, to not expose weakness to the people around me. In Literature, we study Harold Pinter's *The Birthday Party* and talk about the division between public and private personas, and the chaos that results from breaching the divide. The people in DAU are part of my private persona, and so they see my home life.

They see the cycle repeat. As the monsoon starts at the end of each year, my father falls sick and is admitted to hospital. It is almost always a respiratory infection; the white blood cells produced by the donor bone marrow have wreaked havoc in his lungs, attacking and scarring the tissue, making him more vulnerable over time. The last time he is admitted is in November 2010. I ride with him to the hospital. It is my first time in an ambulance.

10:57:42 <ice-evanesco> okay, the doctors just told
my father he may not have long to live.

10:58:05 <DeadRosebud> :(

10:58:24 <alisette>):

10:58:42 <ice-evanesco> the doctor told the family
already, but not my father, so… yes. he may just
lose his determination.

11:01:04 <darkrosefairy77> ice-evanesco: :noes:

11:01:12 <darkrosefairy77> But his stubbornness
is key!

11:01:27 <ice-evanesco> i know. my mom is leaving the office now to visit him.

11:01:45 <ice-evanesco> he might just blow up
at us all, and say that we lied to him and gave him
false hope and stuff.

11:02:19 <darkrosefairy77> ice-evanesco: That is
just the manly reaction to fear

11:02:32 <darkrosefairy77> I really hope he's alright

11:02:58 <DeadRosebud> Same here.

11:03:52 <alisette> Thirded.

11:04:12 <ice-evanesco> darkrosefairy77: yeah,
i hope so too. :huggle: even if it all blows over,
there'll be more storms to weather along the way.

11:05:12 <ice-evanesco> oh the stupid goddamn
drama. i regret wishing for something interesting
to happen all those times in childhood. someone
up there listening, please just give me my boring
uneventful life back. D:

11:05:30 <darkrosefairy77> glares at the powers
that be

11:05:31 <ice-evanesco> darkrosefairy77: :shrug:
she's prepared for something like that to happen.
11:06:10 <darkrosefairy77> ice-evanesco: Doesn't
make it any better. Hug your mum when you have
a chance, yeah?
11:06:52 <ice-evanesco> darkrosefairy77: i will.
i should be going now, but i'm dreading it.
11:07:12 <DeadRosebud> ice-evanesco: :cuddle:
11:07:31 <ice-evanesco> DeadRosebud: :hug:
11:07:35 <darkrosefairy77> ice-evanesco: Well I'm
off for the evening. Best wishes for the rest of your
day love. You can always get a hold of one of us if
you need anything even if it's a hug
11:07:53 <ice-evanesco> darkrosefairy77: i know.
:heart:
11:07:35 <darkrosefairy77> ice-evanesco: :heart:

//

I *did not*, however, post a status update on Facebook. My
Facebook had become a battlefield of sorts, as I had felt *pres-
sured* to add my classmates and bullies as "friends." Facebook
was only just beginning to have privacy settings, but I felt a
need to prove that I was thriving, that I was not suffering the
aftermath of being bullied — the paranoia, anxiety, and depres-
sive urges. Mental health was not a thing that was known; it
was not a thing that was discussed. The only thing we knew
about mental health was that crazy people went to a mental
asylum. I was afraid to slip up, to out myself as being *crazy* and
thus *dangerous* in an environment that emphasised conformity
and results more than individual well-being.

The trap of social media having real-life consequences had closed on me rather earlier than others. The school counsellor had added me on Facebook and was using my social media posts as an indicator of my mental health and "delinquent tendencies" (mostly it was tardiness caused by anxiety-driven insomnia and nightmares). Behind my back, she had reported me to the principal, and I was punished just the year prior. The lesson was learned. I could no longer be honest as I once was, as careless with my words as I once was. As the principal said, "I have eyes and ears everywhere."

It was harsh, painful. On some level, it felt like my sanctuary had been breached. It felt like a home invasion. The internet had been weaponised as a tool against me. No one could be trusted except my fellow denizens of DAUnderworld, my fellow geeks and social misfits, my brothers and sisters.

It taught me to carefully consider the implications of my online words and actions, knowing that they could be given a life of their own, long after I had grown past the point of them being representative of who I am. Additionally, I learned that I had to be discerning and scrupulous with who got to access my information.

//

My father is eventually moved to palliative care. His last meal is a can of Coca-Cola. The last time he is awake is December 2. I have just finished my A-levels. I thank him for fighting for so long, for trying so hard. We cry. I promise to take care of everyone.

Before he goes under again, the sea of morphine claiming him, he asks me the date. I tell him. He asks when December 6 is. That is my aunt's birthday, his younger sister and the donor of the bone marrow within him. I know he intends to make it past her birthday.

"Monday, four more days." I reply. He nods, and closes his eyes, returning to the grasp of sleep.

That night, we stay vigil in the chatroom. My friends hold space. I can't remember what we speak about. I am waiting, waiting.

So is my father. He waits in the hospital for his siblings to arrive. They do, and they speak to him, semi-conscious. He crashes, blood pressure dropping, dropping—

The phone rings, and I pick it up. On the other end, I hear my aunts cry. I think my eldest aunt even screams in her anguish. I know what I must do. In traditional Chinese polytheism, the son is the one to perform all rituals. There is no son, only me.

I light the incense sticks, informing the gods and ancestors that my father has begun the ascent to the afterlife.

After the gods, my DAUnderworld friends are next to know. Condolences flood in, and on my profile, expressions of love.

> **Shroom-diabolique** *Student Traditional Artist*
> Hey, gorgeous.
> *loves*
> Reply | Like Dec 4, 2010
> **Raini-Tempest** *Hobbyist General Artist*
> Mama Dragon gives loves.
> Reply | Like Dec 4, 2010
> **Endorell-Taelos** *General Artist*
> Lots of love.
> Reply | Like Dec 4, 2010

alisette *Hobbyist General Artist*
Loves
Reply | Like Dec 4, 2010
Pbangel16 *Hobbyist General Artist*
Loves to you
Reply | Like Dec 4, 2010
CaptainOzz
Lots of love to you.
Reply | Like Dec 4, 2010

//

A decade on, I've known my friends from DAUnderworld for half of my life, and we've transitioned from DeviantArt to Skype and now to Discord. I am still my truest, best self with them, but I am learning to let go of the deeply engrained caution that my experiences have fostered in me. The process hasn't been easy, but I am learning to allow myself to create openly, to curate my content and to own my experiences.

I watch my cousin as she plays with her mother's iPhone. She is ten this year, and in 2023, she will be the age I was when I discovered DAUnderworld. Thus far, her parents have zealously protected her (and her younger sister's) privacy. There is no doubt in my mind that when they are thirteen or fourteen, they might resent this protection as I once resented my father's attempts at installing parental control on my Windows XP computer. They might perceive themselves to be out of the loop on the latest memes, the shiniest apps, the newest social media.

When she is fourteen, she and many others her age will begin to craft their social media presences (well, those who haven't been subject to their enthusiastic parents creating their social media on their behalf, posting every milestone without their knowledge). She will not have the luxury of crafting an alternate persona like I did. Unlike me, she will not be the pilot of a deep-sea vessel or a cosmonaut. She will not find her people among the alien landscape.

As the adult that I currently am, I hope for her safety on the internet. My eyes have been opened to the hazards that my teenage-self had been blissfully, perhaps willfully unaware of. The part of me that is ice_evanesco, the wide-eyed dreamer running wild, hopes for more. I hope she finds treasure. I hope she finds adventure, sirens, mermaids, selkies, the kraken. But more importantly, I hope she finds her own pirate crew, a band of siblings with bonds forged in blood, who will be there for her, like mine are still here for me.

LIKE A GIRL

Jadzia Axelrod

The day before I got the email, I was considering giving up writing altogether. I had just been turned down for yet another writing job, after a disastrous interview.

"You know, this job is serious," the interviewer said. We had gotten along well at the beginning of the interview, but he seemed concerned about the subjects of my previous writing. "Writing for development isn't like writing. . . " He waved his hand aimlessly, trying to conjure the words he clearly wasn't used to saying. "Wizards and spaceships, and the like."

"I realise that," I said. I was dressed in a brown suit and a deep purple tie emblazoned with a pile of gold arrows that looked as if they had fallen out of Robin Hood's quiver. It was one of my more conservative ties — unlike, say, the one with an airplane dropping bombs emblazoned with bright red hearts — but I wouldn't call it serious. My only concession to serious was my white shirt, which I only wore to job interviews. "I can do my less serious writing on my own time. Put those stories on the internet, in the podcast, whatever."

"On the internet," the interviewer said, leaning back in his chair. "You have a lot of success with that, putting stories on the internet?"

"Sure."

"You've made money, doing that?"

Oh. That sort of success. "Not . . . not really. But some very positive responses."

"Of course. Lot of stories on the internet. Must be hard to find an audience."

"I've always felt that stories find us. People will find my stuff when they need it."

The interviewer did not find this particularly amusing. He leaned forward, his hands steepled in front of him, resting atop the examples of 'serious' work I would be expected to churn out if I was hired. "Let's get back to reality, son. Where do you see yourself in five years?"

I have never known how to properly answer this question. I had tried to make being a freelance writer a viable option, and it wasn't quite working out. This interview, and the many other failed job interviews that proceeded it, was me finally admitting that while writing on the internet was fun, it was ultimately meaningless. There are a lot of stories on the internet. It appeared to be clear that no one would notice mine.

Now, if you had told the me sitting there the truth — that in five years I would be living as a woman, splitting my time being the primary caregiver for my daughter and writing a graphic novel for DC Comics — I would have fallen out of my chair. I would have loved to have claimed that future, but I would never in a million years have imagined that I could. It was too good. So where did I see myself in five years?

"Working here," I said.

I didn't get the job.

What I did get, the day after I considered giving up writing altogether, was an email from a person I didn't know who had heard my podcast story "Hold Me Like A Girl."

//

The thing about writing on the internet is that you are never doing it alone. Writing is, traditionally, a solitary action. The ponderous pace of print publishing means that when your work is finally read, you've already moved on. The piece is more of an artifact of who you were than a reflection of your present state. But, as futurist Clay Shirky once said, publishing used to be a job, but now it's a button. You can launch your writing out into the murky depth of the internet as soon as you're finished, if not before. There's a good chance someone will find it while you're still excited about it.

And there's an even better chance you find some similarly-minded folks who are on the same journey.

My first serious foray into the pixel-stained wilderness of online fiction was founding the website 365 Tomorrows with four other writers (fun fact: two of these five writers later came out as trans). This led me to take up podcasting, creating audio versions of the stories I wrote for 365 Tomorrows. I was part of what I like to call the "Second Wave" of podcasters. If the innovators were techheads and radio enthusiasts, I was part of the group who chased immediately after, excited about the narrative possibilities this medium could create.

This was an era of podcasting when there were so few shows it was possible for there to be a single online directory of them all. And the fiction side of it was a remarkably tight-knit group. We were always helping each other out, filling in for shows, being guests for each other, playing each other's promos. There was a shared community of people working together, trying to get their work out there. None of us were alone.

That's how "Hold Me Like A Girl" came about. A friend needed a story for the next episode of his erotica podcast. I had never written erotica before, but I had an idea that needed an excuse to be written. My wife had told me that I should write about what turns me on. Here would be a chance to do that, explicitly. It was a win for everyone.

All I had to do was write exactly what I wanted to hear.

//

The email itself was innocuous. The author, Cat, talked about her love of podcasts in general before hitting the point of the message: "Of all those many stories that were read to me, "Hold Me Like A Girl" was the sexiest, sweetest, cutest of them all, and its title phrase echoed in the recesses of my mind for all the years since."

Cat goes on to say that she credits "Hold Me Like A Girl" for helping her to realise her need to transition. That what I wrote changed her life "in the most wonderful way possible."

Without meaning to, I had saved her life. By giving a voice to my longing to be a girl, I had allowed her to realise hers.

It would still be years before I saved my own life in the same way.

//

As I embarked on my first journey into creating erotica, I wasn't sure what it was going to be. I was, however, quite sure what I didn't want it to be: I didn't want it to read like a Fictionmania story.

Fictionmania is an online archive of short stories. In a way, it is the democratic dream of the internet made manifest: it is free to use and anyone can submit a story. In a world where so many of the websites of my youth have crumbled to dust, Fictionmania has remained, a monolith of basic HMTL for over twenty years (with the exception of a few outages and domain changes). If you haven't heard about it, it is probably because its massive archive has a singular subject. Fictionmania is a website dedicated to stories about gender transformation.

It is also garbage.

I do not mean that in the guilty pleasure, junk food garbage sense. The stories are trash. I'm not even talking about the often-amateur writing styles. We all gotta start somewhere. But the stories have disturbing veins of racism, misogyny, and all sorts of other problematic stuff. Most notable: a repeated motif is that the protagonist is absolved of any and all agency. Transition happens either accidentally — a lost bet or prank that goes too far, the purchase of a cursed object, or stumbling on alien technology (more common than you might think!) — or it is forced upon the protagonist by someone else. The choice to transition is out of their hands.

Now, this is obviously not a straightforward celebration of unproblematic transness. But at the same time, it's one hell of a potent fantasy. The choice to transition in real life is so difficult to make. Imagine trying to choose between being honest about who you are or to live in hiding. Imagine trying to choose, knowing that the outcome will affect every single aspect of your life. That choice will affect your family, your friends, your employment, your visits to the doctor, your interactions with strangers on the street. Some of that will be for the better, some for the worse, but you don't get to know which cards you're going to get dealt until you sit down to play the game. Away from magic spells and fantastical devices and iron-willed aunts with a taste for extreme corsetry, this choice, it feels impossible. If you've never had to make that choice, you might not understand the appeal of having it taken away.

//

The stories on Fictionmania often emphasise the role of clothing in an erotic context. Unlike having femininity forced upon your protagonist (which, while comforting, is not sexy), the overly-detailed-getting-dressed-sequence was something I wanted to emulate. Even beyond the fantasy of having clothes that fit how they are supposed to, there is a compelling element to the whole business. A striptease in reverse. A costume that reveals your truest self. Wearing a mask so people know who you are.

Not unlike being on the internet. Profile handles and userpics that aren't us, precisely. They're more than us. Us+. Our identity on the internet is the parts of us we wish everyone would see, without the distracting real life stuff in the way: Here is my identity, separate from whatever my parents crafted for me. There is so much overlap between being trans and being on the internet before social media allowed folks in the meatspace to track you down. But you don't have to take my word for it; the Wachowskis made a great documentary about this very phenomenon in 1999 called *The Matrix*.

If that seminal piece of trans/sci-fi/dial tone porn is any indication, the Wachowskis and I think of the internet in much the same way. Namely that it is "dark," despite the fact that, if anything, the internet is made up of light. Softly glowing monitors. Brilliant sparks of electricity racing down cables. From the sickly blink of the LEDs of a dial-up modem to the text notifications that brighten up the face of my phone, the internet is an illuminated presence. But my first experiences with the internet were furtive affairs, done long after bedtimes or with one eye looking out for a teacher. The internet was mysterious, slightly forbidden, and in that way was as enticing as a piece of midnight chocolate.

I tried to create a separate online identity a couple of times. I tried to manufacture a virtual self, a girl who was like me, except maybe more aggressive, more put-together. A girl who knew what she wanted, which felt like the opposite of me in every way.

It's easy to do that on the internet. In that beautiful digital darkness, you are who you say you are. You can put on a mask so people know who you are and you can just as easily take it off again. I'm not the protagonist of "Hold Me Like A Girl," even though they speak of my desires in my voice. I also wrote a story about a man who assassinated the first Tyrannosaurus president. My deniability was plausible.

//

I thought a long time about my response to Cat confessing that my work had changed her life.

Here's what I said:

"I am overwhelmed. Everyone has been touched by a piece of writing at some point, which helped them along the path to becoming who they were meant to be. And every author hopes that one day, something that they wrote will inspire and guide someone else. We hope that, all of us. But I honestly never expected it.

"To have it happen, and to have it happen in this way, is more than I could have ever hoped for. To have played a small role in such a sweet, beautiful event has filled my heart to bursting. I know the journey that led to last night must have been difficult, and I am so happy that you now get to be held as the girl you were meant to be.

"I am especially grateful that your email came today. I have been wrestling with a great deal of self-doubt and frustration with my writing career, and had come to the opinion that my work would never be read, period, much less read by people who it would touch in the ways I hoped. But thanks to you, I see that I needn't have worried. Your story, now, has given direction to me."

Here's what I did not say:

"I'm trans too! What you've achieved is something I long for!!! I just need the strength, do you understand? How were you so strong? How did hearing my story give you strength when writing it didn't do the same for me? Can you help me, the way I helped you? Can you save my life, the way I've saved yours? Please!!?!? I am drowning!!!"

I did not say all of that, because I couldn't.

//

In the years before I received Cat's email but after I had written "Hold Me Like A Girl," I had made a joke at a convention about how podcasting was "disposable culture." I had been podcasting for a few years at that point, and it made sense to me to equate podcasting not to books or to television shows, but to newspapers. Something you experience once and then throw away. Maybe it sticks with you, maybe it doesn't. But for the most part, it's worth about as much as the paper it's printed on. And podcasts, printed on nothing and given away for free, were worth even less.

And yet.

The human voice carries with it an instantaneous, effortless connection that the written word struggles to achieve. There's a feeling of familiarity, of friendship to a voice talking. This is why podcast fans are so devoted. Podcasters aren't just talking, they are talking to you.

A podcast is disposable. Something you listen to once and then throw away.

But that doesn't mean it's worthless.

//

It can be easy to get hung up on assumptions of "quality" in fiction, that stories of a certain caliber are more effective than more amateur variations. That may be true, as far as that goes. But the bar is a lot lower than people think. Careful construction counts, but a story is not a house. It doesn't need to withstand a punishing wind in order to shelter a reader from the storm.

Keep this idea in your mind, this beautiful, egalitarian concept that quality is meaningless when placed against the joy of the human heart. That our emotions, our passions, the very feels that make up all of our lives, each and every one of them, yes, all of them, all of the feels, those matter more than whether a work of fiction is deemed worthy to be remarked upon in a university classroom or any and all of the awards it is eligible for.

Take that idea, embrace it, never let it out of your sight, hold it close to you because my story, "Hold Me Like A Girl"? It's not very good, y'all.

It is, however, written with a lot of feels — mainly longing — and a strong desire to get the slippery genre that is erotica "right," whatever that means. I hadn't written erotica before. I had been told that my writing previously up to this point was clever, but removed. It lacked the tangible passion that comes when one is transcribing their boner, even in a literary fiction mode. I couldn't put what turned me on into words because I knew that once I did, that would make it real.

Not a lot happens in the story. There's no rising action, no action at all, really. There's far too much time spent on the erotic nature of clothing. It doesn't end so much as just stop. The romantic interest is barely sketched out, and the protagonist doesn't do much better.

But there is this part, which I still like, over a decade later:

> For some reason, Brody couldn't look at Freddie.
> "Freddie…a moment ago, on the porch…when we kissed…"
>
> Freddie withdrew his hand. "Didn't you like it? You seemed to like it."
>
> "No, it's not that…" Brody squirmed. Somehow, he managed to turn his face to Freddie. "I…I loved it. Especially…especially the way you held me. I really liked that, the way your arms felt. They, um…it felt like you were holding me. Like a girl."

Freddie slid his right arm behind the small of Brody's back and rested his hand on Brody's corseted hip. His left hand turned its attention to Brody's legs, running up and down the muscular length of Brody's left thigh. "You're more than a girl, Brody. Much more."

//

I am surprised at the bravery I had back then. The audacity to put what turned me on right in the title. What turned me on was being held like a girl. That was what I most wanted, though I could not admit it at the time.

The closest I had come to being perceived as a girl, let alone held, was when I was a teenager in that delightful non-space adjacent to reality, summer arts camp. Despite being outspokenly queer for my entire adult life and closetedly queer for much longer, drag has never been my thing. I wanted it to be my thing. Drag was fun and loud and, most importantly, the performers were seen as women. So when some of my fellow arts camp pals brought up the idea of doing drag for the talent show, I leapt at the chance. Sadly, I was incredibly disappointed to find no dress that fit at the local thrift store. The one I was able to adjust with spare fabric and safety pins to cover my large frame came out looking more comical than anything else. I played up that angle, completing the outfit with garish makeup and light-up deely-boppers. If I was going to look like a laughing stock, I wanted to let everyone know I was in on the joke.

But I wasn't seen as a girl, then. And I certainly wasn't held like one.

This no doubt explains all the attention given to clothing in "Hold Me Like A Girl." Can you even imagine, cute clothes that fit?! Even if you're assigned male at birth? Such luxury! Such fantasy! It's a whole new world!

//

Cat and I are friends now, having found each other again through a mutual acquaintance, yet another writer on the internet who later came out as trans (no, not the one I mentioned earlier, this is a different one. There's more of us than you think). I got her permission to post some of her email, and we talked a little about the whole thing.

"I will be honest with you," I said. "It feels weird to write about a) a real person who b) is going to read this when it's published."

Cat laughed. "I could not-read it, if it helps!"

"No, no. I want you to read it." I said, "I just want to get it right. Get everything that happened right."

"Since we're being honest," Cat said, "It feels mildly weird to be written about — in the 'but I was just being me' sense. But also supremely cool. That you responded kinda blew my mind. I look forward to reading about it from the other perspective."

"You ever think about how that story found you at the right time? Lot of stories on the internet."

Cat paused thoughtfully for a moment. "You ever heard of that expression, the stories we need find us?"

"I've come across it before," I said.

Cat nodded. "I've always liked it. I think it's true. Our stories find us. The internet just helps them along."

I WAS VALKYRIE

Jessica Val Ang

I was in my late teens when a strange and glorious beast was unleashed upon an unsuspecting world, and as an introvert who found comfort in the presence of animals, I embraced it with open arms.

I guess you could say I was slow in developing human-to-human communication skills. I was a quiet and slightly sullen child, often in my own little world in my own little mind. I didn't make friends easily and had difficulty connecting with people. At rowdy extended-family gatherings, I preferred to sit alone with my aunt's fluffy little Pomeranian, playing with him for hours. Other days, I hung out with stray cats, petting them and bringing them tinned cat food, which I bought at the nearby convenience store with my pocket money.

Even as a young adult, I was still trying to find my feet, trying to discover myself and to figure out who I was. Still shy and carrying a lot of subconscious anxiety, I didn't have much of a voice. While I did have amazing friends, I thrived in small groups and

one-on-one. But despite being verbally quiet, I enjoyed being
loud in my fashion choices. I had a dragon tattoo on my shoulder,
back when not many women were sporting any body art at all.
My usual attire was a tiny white strappy tank top, corduroy
bell bottoms, and massive stomper black boots with the word
"DESTROY" across the front. My lips were lined with a dark
brown lip liner, filled with a frosted mocha Revlon Colorstay
lipstick. Yet I was quiet. As quiet as the little girl who played
with stray cats.

That's when the internet interrupted my silent existence.

It was a sudden explosion of instant messengers, chatrooms,
forums, and everything the exciting, mysterious World Wide
Web had to offer. I dived right into it. My dial-up modem was
hooked up to the home phone line that had no call waiting at
the time, and between my brothers and I, the phone was always
engaged by the modem. Mom and Dad were constantly yelling at us to get off the freaking internet. But it didn't dissuade
me from staying up till the wee hours, staring into my laptop
screen, fingers flying over the keyboard as I engaged with my
new-found virtual world. The whirr of tiny plastic fans blowing
on overheating computers in our lovely tropical climate broke
the silence of the night.

One of the first web activities I took to very quickly was
online chatting. Being more of a writer than a talker, I'm one
of those who makes more sense writing a sentence than saying
it out loud. The online chatrooms were the perfect way for
me to start interacting with more people. I began to feel more
comfortable expressing my thoughts and communicating with
other human beings. In the chatroom, everyone was just a name
on the screen. We weren't judged on our appearance or voice;

we had personas built on our words, and through my words, I gained authority. After becoming a regular in the #Singapore channel in mIRC, I befriended the people who were admins of the group, and soon, I was made an admin too. I was taught to use cool scripts to run the mIRC chat program. I became one of the cool kids who ran one of the largest chatrooms on the server, and suddenly, I had a voice. When I spoke, others listened. I was heard and I was respected. My opinions and decisions mattered to a sizeable group, because people knew who I was: I was Valkyrie of #Singapore on the Microsoft/ Galaxynet server.

It was an empowering experience. My authority in the virtual world started to surface in my real-life personality. I started to walk a little taller and speak a little louder. I hesitate to say I found my confidence through an online chatroom, but there was something about those early internet days that made life online different. There was a little more sincerity, a little more authenticity, and a little more heart on its sleeve. Any time of the day or night, I could log into the chatroom and see familiar names there, like Pointblank, Mindslain, rtfm, Catcat, Man-X, and Hansel. We were like family members sitting around the living room in every free moment we had. It was just something we did. It felt like we belonged there. There was a unity and camaraderie that was unique to that era.

Stripped of our visual identities, we only had our words, and so we used our words to share poetry, music, and troubles we were having with people in our lives. Whenever I hear "Perfect Blue Buildings" by Counting Crows, a song we used to talk about, I think about those nights we spent chatting. If I had a bad day in school, coming home to my online fam would cheer me up immediately. We made fun of one another, discussed the latest happenings, and talked about everything and anything under the sun. If a n00b guy came in, asking for a/s/l (age/sex/location), Catcat would change her name to Storm24f and we would have a ball setting him up for a "hot blind date." Through countless hours over long, dark nights, we poured our hearts out to one another. Some of these people I would meet in person, some I would not and never will — like Mindslain, who was a total mystery, yet with whom I had such a close friendship. Those of us who were in Singapore started to meet up regularly in person, for coffee and drinks. I still remember the very first meetup we had. It was a group of twenty of us at a steak place in Marina Square, and Man-X paid the entire bill, much to our surprise. Thereafter, he would frequently take us out, like a big brother, to catch up over drinks and food. When I think about it now, we had so much amazing interaction and sincerity within our group, an experience which has become much harder to find as the internet has evolved.

I went to Australia for my studies in 1999, where the new environment and busier lifestyle forced a change to my habits. It was around this time that I slowly dropped out of online chatting; everyone else also started to move on from chatrooms. In 2004 I came back to Singapore and, as a young adult starting to blossom, I turned to the internet hoping to find a community similar to what I'd found in the #Singapore chats. Looking to find friends, and maybe my partner in life, I started a LiveJournal account.

It started out as a casual, fun diary of my daily shenanigans. People used to stare at me taking pictures of my food with a tiny, discreet point-and-shoot Pentax, not much bigger than my palm. It's so funny how it has become a norm these days. After a few years of food posts and ramblings, the focus of my blog changed when I woke up to see a little spider dangling over me. I put him in a little plastic jar and attempted to get him identified in case he was a stowaway from Australia, as I had just gotten some boxes of my belongings shipped from Melbourne that week. I became fascinated with spiders after trying to find out more. And that was how, in 2007, my Live-Journal evolved into a spider blog, all because of a little web an audacious spider spun over my bed.

I don't know if it was the first of its kind, but I know there were certainly not many spider blogs back then. And unlike the usual insect/spider enthusiast sharing detailed scientific dribble, I was a common layperson who knew nothing, but I found spiders fascinating and slowly learnt more about them. Perhaps that was what drew most people to follow along, because I was a normal girl freaking out over a spider's moult or when a baby spiderling caught its first meal.

It was around this time that I started to make more friends online who were outside of Asia. LiveJournal had a wonderful community-based concept, with a similar sense of the belonging and interaction I experienced in my mIRC days. When we followed people, we actually kept up with each other's lives. We knew and cared about what was going on with one another. We had actual conversations. With real words. Not emoji, not single-word "Amazing!" comments, not by simply pressing the "like" button. "Like" buttons did not exist back then.

This makes me wonder — if "likes" did not exist today, would people be talking more? Back when there was no "like" button, we engaged with one another by actually conversing with words.

It encouraged genuine interaction, and that allowed me to express myself and grow. But as the years passed, developers found ways to increase interaction metrics by creating shortcuts for people to engage with, all for the sake of financial gain. It became all about getting X number of people to see your posts. Yes, the "like" button is very convenient. But it killed genuine interaction. I find myself spending less and less time on apps like Facebook and Instagram. I really miss the authenticity of online communities, but I'm glad I had the chance to experience it, even in the unlikeliest of places. Like an uncommonly genuine and kind community I found just after my spider journey began — an online forum. For purses.

I stumbled across the Purse Forum in 2008, a massive online community of those who, as the name suggests, love purses and fashion. I found it while searching online for ways to authenticate a bag I'd bought. Sometimes I feel a little embarrassed about having been a part of such a "shallow obsession" (a term coined by the Purse Forum), yet this forum has given me many beautiful, life-long connections with women around the world. There's Mica, Liliana, Ro, and Jess from Australia; Sheree in the UK; Vickie, Anna, Leslie, Jennifer, and Char from the US; Mona in Canada; Raquel and Maria in Spain; and many others. We shared information, opinions, ideas, and thoughts, ranging from fashion to health to family and relationships. We gave compliments and support generously. When Raquel was robbed one day and lost her beloved Chloe mini Paddington purse, we all chipped in to buy her a replacement. That was what I loved most about the earlier years on the internet. People were kind. At least most of them were. Or maybe I was really lucky. And when we did come across "trolls," we simply moved

on away from them. We had a support network of positivity
and love, which buffered us through any trouble we ran into.
Gradually, because of my interactions with these amazing
women online, being open and supportive became a part of
who I was offline.

As the years passed and shallow obsessing gave way to other
pursuits, I stopped logging into the forum, but we keep in
touch through other platforms like Facebook and WhatsApp.
Some of my closest friends today include a small group of us
who came together because of a motorcycle jacket. We met on
a thread in the Balenciaga sub-forum, dedicated to discussion
on the Balenciaga classic leather moto jacket. I was starting
to travel more at the time and got myself one of these jackets
to keep me warm on my adventures. Initially, I joined the
discussion to get help on sizing, but everyone was so lovely
to chat with that I stayed. We would share styling inspiration,
pictures of where we were wearing our jackets, and what we
were doing while wearing them. Through this regular sharing, we got to know the daily lives of one another pretty well.
Five of us (Julie from Dallas, Jen from San Francisco, Meg
from Los Angeles, Hilda from Toronto, and myself) started
chatting daily in a WhatsApp group. I met up with Jen in
February 2013 in San Francisco, and again in Taipei just
recently in June 2019 when we both travelled there. Julie,
Hilda, and I hung out in Hong Kong in December 2013 for
meals, drinks, and shopping. Julie and I also caught up for
lunch in Los Angeles when I was there in 2015. I'm looking
forward to visiting Meg when I'm in Los Angeles again next
month. And we have plans to get everyone together in the
near future, perhaps for Christmas.

What started out as a common interest in one leather jacket blossomed into lovely, genuine friendships spanning across continents. Whenever I had any good or bad news, they were some of the first people I'd share it with. It feels surreal that a jacket brought us together. Some days, I don't even remember that.

I feel it's a shame that the online world has changed so much. But I guess it was an inevitable process. That's just like how life is — moving, growing, evolving. I feel glad to have experienced it in its early years and to have met my people in those days. One of the biggest blessings I am thankful for is meeting the love of my life online in 2018. I still wear my heart on my sleeve, as he does, and I believe this made us connect instantly when we met. There is so much wariness in the world these days that when you meet someone open-hearted, you know it like a sudden breath of fresh air. With him, it felt like that. And after a long journey of self-discovery, I was home. We were married last October.

In the fast-moving, fast-scrolling world today, I still try to be genuine in my interactions online. It is so easy to fly through social media and barely spend a second looking at a glossy photo. But life is not about that, is it? What does it mean to us, when we hit that "like" button on a photo or a caption that we won't remember in the next five minutes? Does it really matter? No, the action doesn't matter — but the people do. And the feelings do. And the connections we build do. In a world where many people are spending all of their time and effort trying to get the attention of the rich and famous, I'd take my time to leave a heartfelt comment for someone I actually care about. Not because it's cool to do so, but because it means something to me. Because it's about authenticity.

I am not a religious person. But I do believe things happen for a reason. The internet has played a part in helping me become the person I am today. It gave me a way to develop connections that transcend the virtual world, so I could build my tribe of amazing friends and meet my soulmate for life. It gave me a voice when I had trouble finding it, allowing me to grow strong and be heard. The little girl who preferred the company of animals, although still slightly shy with strangers, is now capable of holding her own.

THE BEAST IN ME

Thomas Pluck

The first time I logged onto a chatroom, I killed the first person I met.

To be fair, this chatroom was a MUD, a "multi-user dungeon" based on fantasy text adventures, so I was forgiven for mistaking it for a game. Later my victim and I would be lovers, and then friends. An odd reversal, but "cybering" — or "tinysex"as chatroom shenanigans were called — was less intimate than divulging personal details, like your name.

The original MUDs were the first MMPORGs, multiplayer text fantasy games inspired by *Colossal Cave*, the first computer text adventure. Sold as Zork by Infocom, it spawned a hundred imitators, and fans of interactive fiction still create and share new games. Some MUDs were timed, and your avatar was supposed to collect treasures, fight monsters, and solve puzzles before the game reset in a number of hours. You could play nice and help other characters or hinder them and compete. Or you could hang around and talk, by typing *say* and words in quotes, such as:

Roxiana says, "Stop looking at my tits, Japhet."
or */em* (short for emote) for actions, such as
Japhet grins. And thinks about them, instead.

The social thing caught on, coders made spinoffs called Tiny-Mucks (a pun on playing in the mud), and all sorts of variants blossomed on secret ports on college servers. On these, you could hold long conversations in virtual "rooms" full of other characters or go off alone as a couple and have cybersex, typing at each other one-handed.

There was a whole host of people I knew intimately back then, everything except for their real names. People like Peganthyrus. Ashtoreth. Misty. I was Japhet, a charming thug brazenly based on James Gandolfini's psychopathic mobster Tony Soprano, and Roxiana, a rapier-wielding fox musketeer who fended off the advances of the over-amorous furries with wit and violence. Life on the MUDs was a book you wrote as you typed, a book you could live in! It was addictive and terrifying.

We lived in those digital worlds practicing different versions of ourselves, learning how to be. We might never know each other if we passed on the street, but in those virtual worlds we shared deeply and personally, things we could never tell family or friends. Family wouldn't understand why you wanted to stay up all night pretending to be a dragon, talking about what new music you downloaded off Napster, your shitty job, or how you were going to pull together a passing grade this semester after skipping your morning classes because you were up all night cybering with Vampire_Lestat, who couldn't get enough of your kitsune werefox wiles.

As long he didn't know you were a guy.

To be fair, I had no way of knowing if "he" was a guy. The classic New Yorker cartoon stated, "On the internet, nobody knows you're a dog." That goes both ways. In the virtual text world of a TinyMUD, if you don't break the spell, nobody knows you're *not* a six-foot-tall swashbuckling pirate vixen.

Some players kept a single persona, but others had a whole brace of them. I had several across several MUDs, from one based on *Vampire: The Masquerade* to the infamous den of the furries, FurryMuck. At one point I ran a private one called GooGooMuck on a server for friends to chat on and share music. We all knew each other's real names by then. Some of us had met IRL and broken the spell, but we still played avatars for the fun of it.

I had cut my teeth roleplaying in high school in a Dungeons & Dragons game, but the furthest I got from myself was playing a Drow elf. Casting spells at umber hulks was fun, but playing a swaggering stud with effortless charm? That was addictive.

Not gonna lie, some of us could write *hot*. No "Worst Sex Scenes of the Year" awards here, with awful mixed metaphors about vaginas gripping you like a pepper grinder. (Google it.) We had plenty of experience reading slash and other erotic fanfiction on Usenet, and most internet citizens were college students back then, so often it was the first time we were away from home, not having to worry about parents barging in to find us writhing in masturbatory ecstasy.

When the movie *Catfish* came out, inventing the term "catfishing," I had to feign surprise when my co-workers professed disgust that someone would pretend to be a different gender on the internet. Because I'd done it for years.

I never used it to con someone like the subject of *Catfish*. On Mucks it was considered rude to ask. Once you knew someone well, you might "talk RL" and break character in private chats. But if it was a tinysex fling with a vampire who wanted to play with a foxy swashbuckling domina, and the person behind the mask just *had* to know her player's gender . . . well, I cut them off. They broke the spell.

I enjoyed playing Roxiana. I did so for almost ten years, and sometimes I slip and talk about her like she's a separate person and not an aspect of my personality, like a drag persona (which she was). She was invented when I found a cheap plastic fox mask in a party store that covered my huge acne-pocked face and walked home from school wearing it, talking to my friend Christian in a lilt. I never did that in public again, but it felt somehow right. Freeing.

I knew what drag was from an early age because my uncle ran a gay bar in Manhattan, and the customers and crew were his second family. He knew Divine. I was taught early what trans meant, because Tom the bartender became Betty, and she was as much family as Sasha the leg-breaking bouncer, who protected the bar from gay-bashing scum. I would never conflate playing a different gender online with being trans or even "understanding" trans people better than any another cis male — but virtual gender-switching is a way to briefly liberate yourself from rigid patriarchal roles.

I am a cis bi male writer, but having grown up IRL with flamboyant gay men, trans women, butch lesbians, and toxically hypermasculine het men, I wanted to *be* all of them. Becoming Roxiana was a form of respectful play, a tribute to women I knew, like my acerbic great-aunt Mary, and Val, the tough

Harley-riding lesbian who opened jars of olives for me at cock-tail parties. I missed my uncle's bar family and their stories. Roxiana was born as much from Jerry, the six-foot queen with a flaming red walrus mustache, as the unapologetically strong women in my family. And she was a lot of fun to be.

That being said, at least three of my online friends from the FurryMuck days transitioned, that I know of. I don't know if playing different personae online was helpful to them, but I imagine it could be. If you changed the sex or gender of your avatar, few questioned it. You could be whoever you wished to be. If one didn't feel right, you could try another. You could even put multiple avatars in the same crowd and talk to yourself, long before this was called sock-puppetry. If you were insecure, you could have one avatar ask an online friend what they *really* thought of that other person — wasn't he a dork?

I had one friend who had a dozen avatars on the same Tiny-Muck, and I'm certain I didn't know them all. He was good at juggling personae, playing them against you. I settled on two, almost diametric opposites, and I kept them far apart. They were masks for me, and sometimes a mask is the truest rep-resentation of who you are.

But they are still armour, and even in a place where you can "be yourself" you could still need protection. Because not everyone's self is quite so cuddly. The Mucks were no online utopia. There were individuals just as toxic as trolls and edge-lords are today, emboldened by their anonymity.

Roxiana got hit on a lot. I learned a lot about male entitle-ment, being her every night for years. There was a tool on the MUD that listed every avatar currently online, with their name, sex, and a short description. The "sex" field was only four characters, but you could extend into the description field, so you weren't limited by the M or F the original coders intended. Roxiana's was "Yes, but not with you."

That infuriated a lot of men.

Complete strangers would "page" me (a private message like a DM, for communicating when you weren't in the same virtual "room"), demanding that I explain why I had written them off out of hand, before even meeting them. "Bitch" was bandied about a lot. Some resorted to begging. Thank goodness the only dick pic they could send was a c==3 if they were clever, and most of them weren't. Also, they *had* to behave.

Because Mucks had something lacking in most corners of today's internet: *moderators*.

They weren't poorly paid, untrained people with no skin in the game; they were players themselves, who cared about the place and keeping it safe. A good troop of moderators kept the trolls at bay. And we were all so addicted to being someone else that the punishment of a ban was terrifying.

As the ultimate punishment, your avatar would be kicked off and re-passworded, and you could never use that name again. But true bans were rare. Someone who made rape threats was banned (imagine that, @jack). But most times you were suspended for a few hours or days to cool off, and it felt like *forever*. You could make a new avatar, but it wasn't the same. If you tried to be cute, and log in as let's say Rox l ana, the community was small enough that mods (called wizards, for their extra "powers") could spot you from the ban list and kick you off with a warning.

This was usually enough to keep the peace, but there were repeat offenders and yes, edgelords, who got their pleasure from taunting others and bending the rules. In the small hours, when most of the mods were asleep — except for one or two who lived on different continents — the trolls would rule.

One of the most infamous was named Random. He was loathed. He had a knack for bullying, knowing what would set someone off. I'm sure he's immortalised in a wiki somewhere as a monster, and I can't say he never said anything bad enough to deserve that. I'm sure he did. He was a sad person who made himself feel better by hurting others. What we call an asshole, in VR or RL.

But we rescued him.

I don't say that mockingly. A mutual friend just would not give up on him. He would taunt her and she wouldn't take the bait, while I would lose my temper. She'd throw back insults at Random even harder. Eventually they became like a fictional couple who trade vitriolic barbs, and when I got tired of the Muck's technical difficulties and hosted my own chatroom, Random was invited.

And he behaved, at least when he was with us. He could've been on other Mucks being nasty to people, but maybe he grew out of it.

Over time, like petting a feral animal, we became friends. He was a hefty guy who loved his cat, lived at home, and used other people as an outlet for his frustrations. He never stopped teasing me for playing Roxiana and TinySexing with guys, but I think he was jealous that Rox always rebuffed his advances and taunts. I was truly sad when his mother posted on Facebook that he died. I made a reflexive social media gesture and told her I was sorry for her loss, but not how I knew her son. She didn't need to know that I only interacted with him online, just that

I cared about him and missed him. I'm sure she was aware that
he typed away long into the night for much of his too-short life.

Random was awful, but the worst thing I ever heard was
from someone who claimed to be a friend, who refused to talk
much about IRL. Once he was down and we tried to get him
to talk, he said:

You're all just words on a screen to me.

It felt positively psychopathic. The majority of my friends
were people I interacted with entirely online. I couldn't grok
that at all, differentiating between online friends and those
you met in person. Eventually I would blur that line and meet
many of my online friends IRL. Some for hookups, others for
friendship. I'm still friends with a handful today, though we
never talk about the times when we played lemurs and vampire hunters by furiously typing in the dark, in dorm rooms or
computer labs.

The mirror-black screens we stare at for much of our lives
reflect our faces like Alice's Looking Glass, and the world on
the other side can be a safe haven for our secret selves. You can
be anyone or anything, if what you type suspends the disbelief
of those who read it. In an online chatroom, it requires consent
and complicity — *I'll believe in you, if you'll believe in me* — to
cast a mutual spell where you can learn to be yourself by pretending to be someone or some*thing* else. A spell that's only
broken when someone is boorish enough to talk OOC — out
of character — and bring you back to the dreaded real world.

We cast this spell together with monochrome text in a Tiny-
MUD chatroom window, waiting for squealing modems to
negotiate first thing in the morning before work or class, to
all hours of the night in college computer labs or darkened

bedrooms. Pretending to be cyberpunk heroines, sexy anthropomorphic foxes, bubble-eyed anime characters, centaurs, brooding vampires, Disney cartoon characters, or creations of our own making. Roleplaying dramatic or silly plotlines, "tiny-sexing," and simply chatting in newly fashioned skins of our own design, where we felt more comfortable than IRL. You say it's not *really* you, but of course it is; perhaps it's truer to you than you've ever been in the presence of another. To paraphrase Oscar Wilde: *Give someone a mask, and they will reveal their true self.*

It's not something I can *talk* about. Write about, yes. Maybe we could text about it? No, we'd recognise the phone number, or our name would show. We'd have to create anonymous email accounts and type in short bursts, in the middle of the night. Watching the cursor blink, as we eagerly awaited each other's replies. Thousands of miles away from one another, communicating at the speed of light.

Then I might feel safe enough to share my most secret self, one more time.

KAYFABE

Kaitlin Tremblay

"Mark's in the hospital."

I remember reading Amanda's message once. Then twice. Then closing MSN Messenger altogether.

I was fifteen, it was the early aughts. Amanda was a person I had met on the internet and never once in real life. We shared wrestling fanfic. We built fan sites together with pictures of the Hardy Boyz, Edge and Christian, and other tag teams made up of handsome best friends that we could imagine going on double dates with.

I told her about how much I hated high school, hated having to make friends with other kids my age after playing on an all-girls baseball team shattered my self-esteem and confidence. Typical angsty teen stuff — probably fuelled by listening to too much My Chemical Romance and Hole — but that was my entire world. I shared the deepest of secrets with Amanda, the secrets that only felt safe shared digitally, with no faces, no voices.

No part of that friendship had ever meant speaking on the phone. If Mark was in the hospital, should I call Amanda? Would she call me? Or would there be a potential plane trip, hours in a hospital waiting room together, no screens or MSN Messenger statuses to buffer our quiet awkwardness (like a choice lyric from Yellowcard's "Walk Away"). Amanda's and my friendship was built on words. Words typed into MSN Messenger chat windows, into emails, into letters. Words typed into fanfics. Words that could allow us to be vulnerable in a detached way, because they never were meant to be any more than that. Words that were just part of stories we were telling each other and ourselves.

Turns out Mark being in the hospital didn't mean any of that IRL stuff happening. Because "Mark" wasn't real. The picture I thought was him was a picture found through Yahoo!, and the person I thought he was turned out to just be a flimsy backstory created by somebody else. Somebody I once spent all of my time thinking about, but who is now just a shadow, a name I had forgotten until now: Catherine. Mark was also just words.

But the relationships around "Mark" were real. And they caused me and Amanda to batten down the hatches, draw inwards, and grow our friendship. What started as conversations about WWE dream teams, fanfic support, and typical teenage angst grew into a supportive relationship between Windsor, Ontario, and Chicago, Illinois; between two people who didn't know how to fit our fleshy bodies into the spaces that were demanded of us, but knew that Dashboard Confessional's "Hands Down" was the best song to put to a fan edit video of Lita's most iconic moves while she was recovering from neck surgery.

//

I was introduced to Amanda by a friend — Nadia. Nadia and I both loved WWE. We watched Raw every Monday night, Smackdown every Thursday, and we would order the pay-per-view every month so that we would never miss an opportunity to cheer on our favourites — and the loves of our young lives — Matt and Jeff Hardy. After all, if we missed out on the latest storylines, how would we ever be able to make sure our fics were cutting edge and pushing boundaries?

Nadia had access to the internet before I did and taught me everything I ever needed to know about building fan sites, sourcing pictures, and most important, forums and fanfiction. My mom had a strict "no chatrooms" policy, but beyond that, I was allowed to use my personal Hotmail and MSN Messenger accounts for whatever I pleased. Eventually that would become using MSN to try to talk to drummers in local punk bands, but for now, MSN was the home of my favourite topic of conversation: Matt Hardy and WWE.

Nadia introduced me to Amanda through MSN, and that's where our tentative friendship began.

> Amanda: Who's your favourite wrestler
> Me: matt hardy
> Amanda: Most people like Jeff tho
> Me: jeffs fine but hes too much for me
> Me: matts way cuter
> Amanda: The Twist Of Fate is pretty cool
> Me: its the best
> Me: too bad they split up
> Amanda: I hate it when tag teams split up
> Me: urs?

Amanda: Edge. Never Christian

Me: edge is canadian

Amanda: That's what Nadia said too :)

At first, I didn't want to share my fics with Amanda. I only showed them to Nadia. I was protective of my writing, worried about if it was bad, worried what other people would think. But Amanda was kind and interested, and I wanted to be a serious writer, and I knew being a serious writer meant being able to let other people read your stories.

My fics usually took the same shape: I was Matt Hardy's manager, helping him book matches to get him en route to a championship title. I was best friends with Kane, and Christian was always a little too weird to be allowed to hang out with us backstage. Eventually, Matt would get the match he deserved, but his opponent (a rotating cast of wrestlers I currently despised with everything my fifteen-year-old body could muster, which, as a femme teen, was a lot) would cheat. Then I'd have to step in, revealing that I wasn't just a manager, but also a spectacular wrestler myself. I'd help Matt win in the ring, then we'd kiss, and everything would be perfect.

Nadia helped me shape my character (and told me it was okay to write myself in, because it was my story, after all), but Amanda helped me write better matches. I'd send her my Word doc, she'd read it, then over MSN she'd give me very thoughtful feedback. How to write with more momentum — how to space out bigger moves, like suplexes and knee strikes, with smaller moves like grapples, taunts, and headlocks, before going back into more electric moves like clotheslines, drop kicks, neckbreakers. If I was a WWE fan — and if cosplaying Lita to go to the movie theatre to watch Wrestlemania is any indication, I definitely was — then Amanda was a super fan. Amanda had movesets memorised, and she could predict which moves would follow which, how storylines would develop, who would have a heel turn, who'd turn babyface, and when a wrestler was being written out due to an injury.

I was in awe of her.

It was Amanda who convinced me to upload my fics online. I remember how proud I was the first time I uploaded one — under my full name, with middle name and all. I felt like a real writer for the first time. This wasn't me writing a "novel" that was essentially just the lovechild of *Baldur's Gate* and the *Dungeons & Dragons* movie, which I made my grandfather read after writing it in a spiral notebook, in pencil, with a printed blurb taped to the back cover. This wasn't a short story about natural disasters that I made my mom read before turning it in as an assignment in grade school.

This was a story I had written and put online for others — strangers — to read. Under my full name. This was it. This was better than being published, I thought, as a prodigy author. This was *real*. Authentic.

I was an author. And Amanda and Nadia helped me get there.

//

Our mutual interests in writing fanfiction and diplomatically different crushes (Amanda always got Edge, I always got Matt, Nadia always got Jeff) naturally dovetailed into real relationships. We'd catch up with each other immediately after Raw or Smackdown ended, updating our MSN statuses to reflect our moods and opinions of the evening's show. We'd share our fics, our theories, and eventually, we'd start sharing small details of our lives. I couldn't concentrate on Raw because I was mad at a math teacher who made inappropriate comments about the length of my kilt. Amanda was having a rough time at her job. (Later, I found out that Amanda wasn't the same age as me and Nadia. She was older, isolated, living with her mom, seeking a similar kind of solitude in talking about wrestling on forums that I was finding talking about wrestling with her.) Our personal lives started becoming more and more prominent in our conversations. True, genuine friendship, all through Hotmail and MSN.

Nadia and Amanda kept meeting more people in different WWE chatrooms, but nobody ever made a deep enough connection with either to really penetrate our protective bubble of three. I never used chatrooms myself, but I never felt like I needed to. MSN gave me all the space I needed to talk, share, and write with others. Amanda and Nadia vetted interesting people who were cool enough to read our fanfic on our custom-made Geocities websites (and who would never interfere with our daydreams by instigating fights we had already decided weren't worth spending the energy over: yes, the Dudley Boyz were fine, but we liked who we liked; yes, Trish Stratus was also beautiful, but we loved Lita, thank you very much; yes high-flyers have a higher risk of injury, but The Swanton Bomb looked really, really cool). We were safe, we were happy, and we were getting along perfectly fine.

So when "Mark" showed up, after an introduction and a vouching for by Amanda, I was a bit surprised. And the fact that Mark didn't show up alone, but instead with two of his best friends, should have been the real warning. But I was young,

I was trusting, and I was beginning to feel unsatisfied with only ever writing about being kissed and never actually *being* kissed. I was getting tired of writing romances for myself with characters that I knew weren't reflective of the actual people playing them. Fantasy was starting to not be enough for me. So I didn't question it when a young, attractive boy (according, at least, to the picture I was shown by Amanda) wanted to be friends. Even if it was through MSN and Hotmail, he'd be writing the romantic words to me, instead of me imagining them. And after all, if Amanda knew him and his friends, then surely he was worth also knowing?

I don't remember the two names given to images found on the internet of the other two random guys, but I do remember this: there was somebody for Amanda, somebody for Nadia, and Mark for me. Just like in our fics, we all had somebody — and they were all friends, just like Amanda, Nadia, and I were. Standard fairy tale stuff, if my fairy godmother was a middleweight wrestler who preferred soaring from the top rope.

With Mark, it started with sharing fics through Hotmail, then grew into long emails to each other when we weren't on MSN at the same time, then escalated into immediately jumping onto MSN after Raw or Smackdown ended to share our thoughts on the night's show. Mark was kind, funny, and most importantly, he liked my writing. So when, after a month or so, he told me he liked me and wanted me to be his girlfriend, there was no way I was going to say no. Sure, we had never met IRL, and he only shared one picture with me — compared to the dozens Amanda shared of herself and that Nadia and I took together and shared with her — but it felt real. It felt like that lonely part of me that was desperate to feel pretty, to feel popular, to feel wanted was finally being fulfilled.

//

It's not even possible to fully remember how I felt about Mark, because those emotions are tied up in a lot of other complex feelings. Betrayal. Fear. Trying to understand the word "catfishing," and then trying to internalise what that meant. Everything I felt was probably real. I remember spending all of my time talking to Amanda about how happy I was, and for a while, I even stopped writing fics. I had something else now to occupy all of my waking thoughts. I didn't need to write fantasies where talented men fell in love with me. All of a sudden, I had that as my reality. I had to have been actually happy, but I don't remember that.

But I do remember exactly how I felt when I read "Mark's in the hospital."

Terrified. In every possible part of my body, I was scared. I wish I had been suspicious. I wish I hadn't immediately believed it. But I wasn't, and I did.

The first thing I did was tell my mom.

My mom knew about my budding friendship with Amanda. When Amanda messaged me to tell me about Mark, I told my mom in secret, away from my brothers. I don't think I asked her for anything. Or maybe I asked her for everything, and was furious when all my requests were denied.

She was tender with me, but firm. Nobody was flying anywhere, but I could make a phone call to the hospital.

When I pressed the other guys — Amanda and Nadia's guys — for a hospital phone number and got silence, we all began to understand. We asked for updates and got silence. We asked for the name of the hospital and got silence. We asked for anything, even just a "hello" back. And we got silence. It all made a sort of sickening sense.

Mark wasn't real.

None of them were.

And this lie, this story, was suddenly too much for whoever was spreading it.

Amanda found the numbers of hospitals in the city that "Mark" said he lived in and called all of them (she lived in the States, so the phone calls were less expensive for her to make). We got nothing. We scoured the news. No reports of an accident that matched the description of Mark's supposed accident. Amanda never stopped looking, and I never stopped appreciating her energy, even though we both were slowly accepting the truth. I think we needed to turn over every stone in order to prove it ourselves. Any idea, any lead, no matter how ridiculous, contained the possibility of the truth: Mark was real and he was hurt and he was somewhere. We just needed to find him.

Eventually, we got a response on MSN. At first it was a friend request, but not from a name we knew. From a teenage girl named Catherine. Said she knew about "Mark."

"It was a joke. I'm bored of keeping this up," she said. Then deleted us from her contacts.

And that was that.

//

Amanda went quiet.

Nadia and I were too embarrassed to speak in person about any of this.

I went on vacation with my family to Florida, met a drummer there (apparently, fifteen-year-old me cared about exactly three things: dragons, WWE, and very cute drummers). He kissed me, and I wanted that moment to be the only thing I ever experienced for the rest of my life: the hot sun, made all the worse by my oversized black jean shorts, leather wrist cuffs, and impossibly long Avril-Lavigne-style hair, him gently rubbing my arms before kissing me. We were on a beach, we had spent the whole day adventuring in the city together, and he was leaving the next day. I tried to write a story about it on the car ride back to Windsor, but couldn't. Every word I wrote about it felt hollow, cheapened by my trying to put words around it. So I let it go. I started listening to Less Than Jake at his recommendation then let it all fade into memory.

I returned to my home in Windsor to emails from Amanda. She was angry after the Mark incident, after finding out Catherine fabricated all these lies seemingly to torture us, but probably just actually out of boredom. While we were writing stories about wrestlers falling in love with us, Catherine was also writing stories about fake love. Amanda was hurt. She felt betrayed. She felt stupid. She wanted to know more about Catherine, but Catherine was even less real to us than Mark or any of them had been. The others were at least stories, names associated with conversations, ideas, emotions. They were real in that sense. But Catherine was actually the real person, and we knew nothing about her. We couldn't find anything out about her. She simply stopped existing after that one message. Amanda was lost. And she was lonely.

And she missed me.

I think her and Nadia stopped talking. Nadia and I began hanging out with different people at high school, and were drifting apart in our own way. Everything was different then. But Amanda and I had each other still, and one thing was for sure: we weren't going to process any of this alone.

My friendship with Amanda would only last another year or so. I started to find new friends, started to realise that while I didn't know how to forge friendships with girls, I was definitely interested in kissing them. I began to lose interest in WWE. The Hardy Boyz were hitting difficult points in their lives and were no longer the bastion of brotherly support and love that Amanda, Nadia, and I had connected with so deeply.

But after the Mark incident, and before I started smoking weed and making out with girls, Amanda and I became the closest we ever were. We stopped talking about WWE altogether. I wasn't watching, and we quickly realised we were more interested in unpacking our feelings of grief, anger, hope, and all the weird, seemingly unprocessable emotions that arise from the pain of being so deeply betrayed. We became invested in each other as people, and not just as characters in our fanfics.

We stopped talking on MSN as much, and our conversations turned into in-depth letters. Maybe we didn't trust the internet after the Mark incident. But even still, we knew we weren't abandoning each other, and we weren't letting this incident fester emotionally. So we wrote each other letters.

I also started writing poetry and shared that with her instead of fanfics. It was easy to be honest with her in my poetry, because she didn't need anything explained to her. She understood the hurt. And she didn't judge my terrible metaphorical attempts. Eventually I'd write a short story about the whole experience and it would be my first-ever published short story, but that would come years later. Until then I'd write bad poems that were titled after the names on paint chips ("Aspen Fog" being the most notable) because they sounded calming, and because I didn't know how else to process what had happened. Writing was harder when it wasn't just fantasy. Kayfabe was easy when it was about how audiences bought into wrestling's fantasy as reality, and not a tired metaphor for my own life.

We created a judgment-free zone where we could write about what happened and where no emotion was "too much." And it helped. It healed.

And then we moved on.

//

I don't talk to Amanda anymore. Part of me used to wonder if she was really Catherine, orchestrating everything. To be honest, I'm still not sure. Looking at this as if it's a story, it makes sense that she would be the ultimate villain here. The most epic heel turn of all time.

Then there's the other part of me that doesn't think that's possible. To be so vulnerable with me the way Amanda was — she couldn't have been lying, could she? Yet she did introduce me to Mark. She handled the phone calls to the hospital. It's all too distant to remember properly.

Now, I don't really think it matters to me either way. Amanda, Mark, Catherine. None of it matters anymore in the same way it did back then. The feeling of betrayal, isolation, paranoia, and the lack of evidence to anchor my fear and suspicions on propelled me down a dangerous path. Underage drugs, friendships with older, predatory men. The closest I ever got to talking aloud about Mark and Catherine was in a priest's basement, learning how to talk about my pain in such a way that would inspire other confused and lonely teenagers to open their hearts and to join Father Mark's group (alright, so maybe I joined a pseudo cult after I stopped talking to strangers on the internet, but in my defence, being a teenager is extremely difficult).

But I did learn how to connect to other women through my friendship with Amanda. With Nadia, the friendship was always strained. Competition, jealousy, aggression. Emotions we didn't know how to process and weren't old enough yet to understand how to give space to. So at a time when I was feeling ostracised from friendships with other girls, I found acceptance, shared giddiness, love, and understanding with Amanda, somebody who could be reduced to just having been a complete stranger on the internet, but who was more than that. It was a friendship I could only find through writing, and through the weird way writing creates both a safe distance and an intense intimacy. We wrote fanfics, yeah, but we also wrote our own stories in emails, in letters, crafting a version of ourselves and what happened that let us find some semblance of ease.

Now, as an adult, there's a lot that I've taken from that friendship. An understanding of the need for community. I've grown into somebody who understands the importance of my friendships, who understands that supporting and uplifting each other is how we become stronger, how we grow more meaningful relationships, and how we can fight to make sure everyone is safe, included, and thriving. How we can't survive our own pain, our own traumas, without this support. I've grown into a community organiser, a friend. A writer. Everything I wanted to be when I first met Amanda.

Recently, I had a conversation with a friend who is also a writer. She was talking about the pressures of being a woman writer in an industry with mentors who are mostly men. About striving to find an authentic voice and career trajectory that doesn't feel harmed by things we can't control (our looks, our bodies, and other people's perceptions of those). About craving a role model or mentor who looked like us, had similar experiences to us. Who fought the same fights we did, and who won. Or who lost, gathered their strength, and learned how to fight stronger, smarter. A conversation many of us have had, in many different ways, with many different people.

But in this conversation, she mentioned how much she missed writing fanfic. Not just for the subject, but for the community around it. For the other women who taught her the ropes of fanfic writing — thus forming the bones of her very successful writing career. These women who also called her shit out, who nurtured her as a writer and a person, showing her how to grow, how to improve, and how to do it all without the pressure of competition and ego.

I responded to her story with something a woman had said in a group therapy session I was in once: "It's nice to be held by other women."

"That's it exactly," she responded.

She was missing this community of women writers who held her.

And while there are days where I remember the year I spent getting to know Amanda, writing WWE fics together, and everything we went through because of Catherine, the happiness I feel isn't hollow. That feeling of companionship, of support, of love, have all been translated into the communities I'm a part of now — communities that are IRL, but importantly, are also still on the internet. Because even now the internet is still a formative place to me as a writer. These online communities — filled with friends, acquaintances, strangers — are still where I can share ideas, challenges, successes, and where I can still grow as a writer. Where we can band together during hard times and cheer each other on during the good times. Where we can share our 3 a.m. thoughts on writing or our tips for surviving imposter syndrome. And where I can still go to get feedback on whether or not it's better pacing to have a clothesline before a DDT or sometime after, when the viewer isn't expecting it.

THE DIGIDESTINED

Charles Pulliam-Moore

The average child of the 90s will tell you that the *Digimon* franchise was a mildly successful, flash-in-the-pan attempt at tapping into the same adolescent frenzy that turned Nintendo's Pokémon into one of the brands that shaped the decade, and for most people, that's exactly what it was. But when I first met the DigiDestined — coincidentally at the same time I was getting my first taste of the internet — it became so much more than just a show. It was a reason to get up on Saturday mornings. It was the beginning of my lifelong, unhealthy obsessions with anime and technology. It was the thing that taught me how deliciously intoxicating it can feel to give yourself over to the almost fanatical obsession that comes with being A Fan™ of something you're supposed to have long-since gotten too old for. It was also the first thing that made the social media-driven digital world we all live in today feel like something that could become real — that was going to become real.

Digimon were collectible toys and mascots who dominated Saturday morning TV blocks, sure, but in the world of the show, they were the bridge between a group of misfit kids and a reality defined by digital information. The brilliant thing about the original *Digimon* series was that its basic premise was just reasonable enough to sound plausible to the right kind of imaginative kid who had too much unsupervised access to the family computer after school. Soon after arriving at their real world summer camp, seven kids (the "DigiDestined") are sucked into the Digital World, a place where reality itself is composed of living, breathing data, and they befriend a series of Digital Monsters as part of their quest to save both worlds, which are linked to one another. *Digimon* was just a cartoon, but the idea that I could leave everything about my boring, meatspace life behind at the drop of a hat because it was my destiny lit my imagination on fire.

The DigiDestined were initially presented as your prototypical anime protagonists who were literally destined for greatness. Which was sort of like my situation. I was too young then to understand that being in my school's computer-centric "gifted" program really only meant that I could read and write at a marginally more advanced level than the school board assumed kids my age would. But on some level, everybody instinctively knows that being in those programs doesn't exactly mean much. Just like in *Digimon*, when the children learned that the real reason for their being called to the Digital World is that they all happened to be awake during a massive Digimon battle in the real world while everyone else in the city slept, everyone in the gifted program may have been "special," but we still spent hours doing the same typing exercises, wandering off into the

Windows 95 games tab to fire up 3D Pinball, and generally being bored.

But in the world of *Digimon*, computer screens weren't just these static hunks of plastic and glass that you sat in front of to learn about far-off places. They were literal portals into another world where your sole purpose was to explore and get lost, looking for the weirdest, coolest things you could possibly imagine. If *Digimon* had ever managed to become as popular as *Pokémon*, it might have been easy enough to get a group of friends into involved explorations of the Digital World on the playground during recess, but no one else I knew was really into the show or felt the same kind of deep compulsion I did to escape into a fictional reality. I was a painfully shy kid who could feign being an extrovert even though it never felt like I was being honest about myself when I did. *Digimon* spoke to me because it was a show about a bunch of kids who had to figure out who they were in order to save the world, and the more I watched it, the more I felt a connection to its characters — like Tai, the team's jocular, strong-willed leader, and Matt, the moody loner who secretly longs for deeper friendships.

I didn't really know how to express my passion for the show to my actual childhood best friends because it all felt too personal and weird. It was one thing to like a cartoon about fighting monsters, but it was another to talk about how easy it was to relate to *Digimon*'s storylines about loneliness and feeling like you don't measure up to your peers. It was something else entirely to admit that even though I knew *Digimon* was just a cartoon, I wanted the Digital World to be real, and every time a computer screen would flicker or a digital clock would suddenly begin acting up, there was a part of me that thought, "This is it. It's gonna happen."

The few times I came close to opening up about any of this with friends, I got the kinds of bemused looks that said, "Hey, we're still cool and all, but let's get back to reality." And that makes sense because no, kids don't get sucked into computer screens, and the virtual pets living inside Tamagotchis don't lead rich inner lives that we don't know about. But *Digimon* invited me to wonder — what if they did? What if there was something more to *Digimon*'s fantasy that you could only glean by really, really, committing yourself to learning everything there was to know about the Digital World the way the DigiDestined had?

The Digital World being a secret that the DigiDestined kept between themselves made it that much more fun to fantasise about being one of them. I knew how ridiculous the idea was on its face, which is why I'd never admitted it to anyone in person, but it was also because keeping that kind of truth about your-self hidden was party of *Digimon*'s mythology. Even though I didn't personally know anyone else who felt the same way I did about *Digimon*, I knew that the show wasn't coming back season after season just for me. There had to be other people watching it with the same kind of passion I felt. The key was knowing where to look, and the most logical place to start was on the internet itself.

For years after *Digimon* first aired here in the US in 1999, I lurked in the shadowy corners of different message boards that occasionally gave rise to impassioned discussions about the show and the collectable toys associated with it that never seemed to be in stock in local stores. One of the difficult parts of getting sucked into dubbed anime in the 90s was living with the knowledge that there *were* subsequent seasons, but there was no way of being certain when — if ever — you'd actually be able to watch them on TV. These days, it's easy enough to log on and just seek out any one of the dozens of fan sites and blogs dedicated to tracking a series' progress as new details are announced and trailers are released. Back then, though, the only thing you could really do was go looking for forums where people with a direct connection to Japan would upload scans of anime magazines where announcements about new series were made. If you were lucky, the scans would be accompanied by translations that gave you just enough information to make sense of whatever you were looking at, but often, character reference sheets and concept art were more than enough to get me hyped up.

At first, the lurking was just a necessary part of figuring out when the show was coming back and learning about the differences between the English dub and its Japanese counterpart. But *Digimon* news always came in irregular fits and starts. For every day when the fandom was alight with information about new species of Digimon, there were weeks when people spent their time just hanging out with one another shooting the shit.

It didn't occur to me at first why anyone would bother getting into threads about sharing what was going on in their personal lives or what music they were listening to at the moment, because I hadn't had an experience that made other people on the internet feel "real" to me. But then in 2003, I stumbled upon With the Will, one of the biggest *Digimon* forum communities, which quickly established itself as the go-to hub for people like me who'd quietly kept their love of the series alive in secret. It changed my life.

I joined With the Will after an intensely bad experience with a torrenting site left my hard drive corrupted to hell, which led to being grounded for a week and forced to figure out a better way of getting my hands on subtitled episodes of *Digimon Frontier,* which wasn't airing in the US yet. With the Will had been around for a few months at that point, and even though the site was still new, it quickly became a central part of how I used the internet. Even if I wasn't actively looking for anything *Digimon*-related, typing in the forums' URL became a reflex borne out of constantly checking the site, and that habit brought me to With the Will just when its members were beginning to coalesce into a community.

To be honest, it was a little disappointing to learn that my intense emotions about a somewhat obscure cartoon weren't quite as unique as I'd once thought, but there was something exhilarating about realising that there are a bunch of weirdos out there just like me who came away from *Digimon* with similar feelings about the show and its characters.

As I got older, we moved multiple times for my mom's job, and it became harder and harder for me to find a place in new social groups and feel like I belonged. I got used to being the new kid because that's just what you do, you adapt. And to be fair, there are perks to being the newbie. People think you're interesting because you're from a different school, which might as well be another world. You're different and strange, and you bring something new into the fold, but at the same time, there's a weight that comes with being the new kid, because you're either always going to be the shiny new thing from some other place, or you have to fight to find a place for yourself in the group where you fit and people want you to fit.

To complicate things, I was also growing more and more certain that the romantic feelings I had for other boys and certain masculine, muscular Digimon weren't going away any time soon. I can look back now and laugh about all of this, but at the time, admitting that I felt that way to anyone seemed impossible because I definitely wasn't going to talk to other kids about it, and as understanding as my mom was, I didn't feel comfortable admitting any of this to her, either.

I never opened up about how much the "new kid identity" weighed on me until I started posting on With the Will. There, almost everyone immediately understood where I was coming from, either because they'd gone through similar things, or because they'd seen stories like mine play out in *Digimon* itself.

When the DigiDestined weren't duking it out with the forces of evil, they spent a lot of their downtime in the Digital World coming to grips with personal demons they assumed they'd left behind in the real world, like their fears about death and their feelings of inadequacy. Each season of *Digimon* was different than the next, but the show never failed to feature an extended arc about an outsider DigiDestined, one who joined the team late into the game after spending a considerable amount of time acting as a villain before learning the error of their ways and owning up to the fact that they just want to be included. Those were the things about *Digimon* that spoke to me but, being a teen, I was scared at first that being honest about where I was at emotionally would set me up for social failure on the forums. I wanted people to think I was cool and edgy and only had deep, ruminative thoughts about *Digimon*'s dense lore. But the more I read With the Will, I saw how people in the forum were with one another. There was playful teasing and people would get into heated arguments with one another, but there was also an open earnestness to everyone's interactions that felt like a foundational part of the forum's culture. No matter what kind of person you were or where you were coming from, if you loved *Digimon* and introduced yourself to the forum specifically for new members, there would be someone online to welcome you in and let you know that you'd found a place for people like you.

I don't remember exactly what I said in my first post, but I remember being nervous about saying that *Digimon Tamers*, the third entry into the franchise, was my favourite because of the way that it followed a character's descent into a deep, existential depression. I didn't think those kinds of themes would really resonate with other people the way that they had with me, but a few anxious minutes after I hit "submit" and my post went live on the site, a response came in. And then another, and another, and eventually the thread was full of people I'd never met telling me that they'd all felt the exact same way and emphatically agreeing that *Digimon* had really taken a downward turn after *Tamers*.

Before With the Will, I couldn't fathom ever being open about how blindsided I was by a *Digimon Tamers* plot that focused on Jeri, a member of the DigiDestined (that's not what they're called that season, but roll with me), sinking into a world-ending depression after she's forced to watch the violent death of her partner Leomon. Previous seasons of *Digimon* had always been careful to remind you that no matter how violently a Digimon "died," their data would eventually end up being reformatted and the Digimon would be born anew. But in the world of *Tamers*, things were different; Digimon fought to consume one another in order to become more powerful, and Leomon's death was permanent.

You weren't supposed to have feelings that earnest and raw about fictional, anthropomorphic animals. But on With the Will, everyone understood how devastating the death was and how the series' decision to make its characters live with that finality marked a pivotal turning point in *Digimon*'s evolution. Feeling all of your feelings out in the open wasn't a With the Will requirement, but it's something moderators encouraged by urging people to be themselves and swooping in whenever a thread got too pointedly spicy at any specific person's expense. With the Will was a place where everyone felt comfortable being their truest, dorkiest selves and talking about *Digimon* things that we'd always felt too uncomfortable to discuss with people in real life. We could all be honest about how absurdly sexualised so many of *Digimon*'s Catholicism-themed, angelic monsters like Angemon and Angewomon were and how the series' creators weren't at all concerned about channelling their personal kinks into their work. Talking about my own queerness in the forum was surprisingly easy because of the way other people were open (if kind of awkward) about their sexualities in a way I couldn't imagine my friends being with me in real life. The more I opened up in the forums, the more I realised that of course I wasn't the only gay kid who had complicated feelings about the muscular, humanoid Digimon who were obviously designed by illustrators who had a thing for fetish gear. I'd always thought that I was the only person who found angel monsters in garters and bustiers kind of weird-hot, but people talked about the fuckiness of *Digimon*'s aesthetic with a casualness that made it clear that I wasn't alone. It wasn't so much that *Digimon* awakened anything in me — I'd known I was gay for a while at that point — but it felt good to see some of the same kinds of feelings I had being understood by people I considered friends, even if I never planned on meeting them in person.

Even though the forums were a place where everyone got along in theory, the same social norms that cause people to seek out others similar to them IRL carry over into digital spaces. People who were strict about grammar tended to gravitate towards each other in the same way that the soundtrack-obsessed music geeks would cluster. Learning those new rules felt tedious at first, and I often found myself wondering what I was getting out of poring over badly translated transcripts of Japanese audio drama CDs in order to understand whether someone's argument about the extended canon held any water. But the more accustomed I became to the general atmosphere of the forums, the more natural that kind of exhaustive close reading of *Digimon* as a text felt, and this led me to carve out a space for myself and find my people in With the Will's roleplaying section.

The impact roleplaying had on shaping With the Will's culture isn't really something that can be understated, because the roleplaying threads were a place where you could really get a sense of what kinds of people the forum attracted. But that reality was intensified by the fact that we weren't just roleplaying any old random series with digital strangers: this was *Digimon* roleplay — roleplaying about people for whom the internet was a physical space where their dreams could come true.

Knowing that other people in the forum were just as into the idea of slipping into a fantasy Digital World of our own making

made it easy to talk about the real-world things I couldn't articulate to my friends and family offline. Online, I didn't need
months to muster up the courage to come out to anyone, because
you never had to wait too long for the topic of *Digimon*'s homo-
erotic subtext to organically come up in casual conversation.
Even though our scenes could go on for days, they never exactly
went anywhere, because we all knew that that wasn't the point.
On some level, we all implicitly understood that the reason we
kept the scenes going and began new adventures when we got
bored with the old ones was that we were all owning up to the
fact that we wanted to be like the DigiDestined. We wanted
to be called upon to save the world because the sheer power
of our emotions made us special.

It feels weird to think of it this way now, but everything
I know now about scoping people out from the safe distance
afforded by the internet, I learned by getting caught up With
the Will's roleplaying threads. No matter how thoughtful
and nuanced your contribution to a scene was, it was all for
nothing if you couldn't follow the thread creator's guidelines
for gameplay, or if the guidelines you set up didn't seem well
thought-out. People revealed what kinds of storytellers they
wanted to become and what kinds of storytellers they actually
were through those threads, and seeing them shift into those
different versions of themselves, slightly adjacent to the people
you knew from the news and *Digimon* speculation threads,
was enthralling.

The forum never exactly felt like a place where I went to
hide from the world, but it was a distinctly compartmentalised
part of my life that I wanted to keep separate from everything
else because it was the first place where I was able to present

and inhabit a completely constructed version of myself. Met-aphorically trying on new hats is a part of growing up that gives you a sense of the kind of person you want to be and the kind of thoughts and feelings you want people to associate with you. Even when I wasn't fantasy roleplaying, every one of my forum posts was a performance of a version of myself that didn't really exist offline, at least not yet. In the real world, my politics weren't fully formed back when the forums were a big part of my life — I wasn't that kind of kid. But politically charged threads debating the most recent election none of us had been old enough to actually vote in gave me a space where I could feel myself beginning to develop a more nuanced and clearly defined worldview.

In person, the process is slow and complicated by more factors than you could ever hope to take into account, but it's different when you're expressing yourself with your words on a screen. Hopping back and forth between threads and private messages meant having to know how to shift between alternate versions of myself — the roleplayer, the debater, the mediator — with fluid ease. After a while, it became second nature, and it would be years before I realised that what I was doing wasn't at all weird, but rather learning how to maintain multiple senses of self at the same time. Feeling that way gave me the sense that I knew myself in some deeper, more profound way that never could have happened if I hadn't pushed myself to dive into the forums with the goal of understanding and finding my place in them.

With the Will taught me almost everything I needed to know about maintaining an online presence right at a time when social media with a direct connection to my real-world life was beginning to shape my social landscape. I say almost because I didn't and still don't really know how to say goodbye to social platforms in ways that make it obvious I'm through with them. There was never any one particular incident that nudged me towards thinking that it was time to leave, but my getting older and *Digimon*'s decline in popularity played undeniable roles in my gradual withdrawal from the community. Even though the explicit text of the series had long since stopped being the primary reason that most people still logged in each day, it had always been a familiar part of our digital atmosphere. It reminded everyone why we originally started frequenting the site and, without it, it was hard not to be drawn away by the wild, uncharted digital territory Facebook and Twitter were opening up to the world.

I don't remember the last time I punched in my long-forgotten username and password into With the Will, but I know that one day, I looked up and saw that nearly every person online was someone I didn't know and, while the site was chugging along the way it always had, it didn't feel like the home I'd known before. The forum had changed, I'd changed, and that was okay because I'd gotten what I needed and then some. I joined With the Will because I never wanted to have to wait to know how *Digimon* was complicating and reimagining the ideas that first made me fall in love with the series as a kid, but I walked away from the forum with a better sense of my own mind and what having a meaningful connection to a fandom could truly feel like.

'NIICHAN

Mel G. Cabral

The car swerves violently through the parking lot. *I never asked for any of this to happen*, she shouts, banging her fist on the steering wheel, *never asked to have children that treat me so.* She sniffles, one of the few times I've ever seen Mom weep. I want to tell her, *I only fight with him because he hurts you so.* I grip the passenger-side ceiling handle, fearing for my life, wishing I had a phone, a laptop, *anything* that could let me escape even briefly from the confines of this car. I wish I could reach for my friends across the world, wish I could tell them everything I can't say, wish I had my 'niichan with me, instead of being on our way to get my so-called brother, whom I haven't even seen in six years. All I can do is shut my eyes and plug my ears with earpods as we reach the pick-up point and let Jerry into the back of the vehicle and back into our lives.

//

I remember the year 2000 not for the Y2K Scare, or for the fact I turned ten or found my first fandom, but as the year my brother Jerry migrated to London to earn a master's degree in business. After we dropped him off at the airport, I quickly took to the internet to tell my online friends, who responded with *confetti* and *party poppers*.

I don't remember if I ever told anyone else about it. Probably not my friends at school, who were mostly my friends by circumstance. I was a huge fan of anime, manga, and video games — hobbies which disinterested most of my schoolmates. I didn't know any of my neighbours, much less anybody outside a couple kilometres' radius of my house or my school. I didn't have much of a choice: my mother refused to ever let me leave the house on my own, insisting that she or our *yaya* — the local Filipino term for a person hired to help around the house and with the family — always accompany me as my guardian. When I'd ask to join my friends at this or that event, my *yaya* would huff and tell me friendship was pointless. If my friends invited me to their houses, my mother insisted on having *them* come over instead (but then being incredibly picky about who she let into the house). It led to a lot of teasing at school, being called a mama's girl, being told that I was a spoon-fed baby who couldn't fend for herself. I never even had my own bedroom, instead sharing one with my mother as I was growing up. My life back then tended to be like this:

1. Wake up at home
2. Get dropped off by *yaya* at school
3. School
4. Get picked up by *yaya* at school

5. *Yaya* accompanies me to the mall next to our house
6. *Yaya* accompanies me home after the mall

An endless cycle of isolation and loneliness. The only other flesh-and-blood people around me were *yaya*, my mom, and Jerry.

Jerry is thirteen years older than me. He graduated from business school as a university scholar and worked for a couple of years in a prestigious local bank. On the side, he liked to think of himself as a poker expert, gambling in a few casinos offline and online. Jerry had terrible eyesight, a massive complex about being short (which he eventually got cosmetic surgery to correct), and an unfortunate skin condition called eczema. My mother tried everything she could get her hands on to provide him some relief from the eczema, but nothing worked. When he was itching, he constantly snapped at us, and whenever we'd offer advice, he'd tell us we knew nothing before storming off, only to return doing exactly what he had been told to. He'd scratch himself so badly and so often, he'd have broken and bleeding skin. My mother scolded me every time Jerry and I got into a fight, despite Jerry being the one to start it, and despite me only butting in because he was yelling at her. She always defended his behaviour, asking me to be more understanding of him, insisting that there was still a good, loving *kuya* buried somewhere underneath all of that insufferable asshole. *He's just teasing you*, she'd say, *it's his way of showing affection for you*. If it was being in constant pain from eczema, or his low self-esteem about his height or eyesight that prompted his nasty behaviour, I'll never truly know. But what I do know is that Jerry made my life a living hell.

Jerry would constantly tease me about being overweight, overwrite the save files on my PlayStation memory card with his own, and insist that he was right and I was wrong. My mother's response was to sign me up for a gym membership, buy Jerry his own PlayStation, and tell me to stop being so stubborn. Every single time my brother managed to get under my skin, he would give out a loud, booming laugh, one that lasted for what felt like the longest seconds of my life.

Even when he kept his mouth shut, it was hard to ignore his presence. I'd hear the scritch-scritch-scratch of his nails against his skin as he passed me in the dining room. A strange and overwhelming smell of who-knows-what (testosterone?) would waft into my nostrils whenever I had to retrieve something from his room. I dreaded the sound of his footsteps, our bedroom door inevitably slamming open at 3 a.m., his angry barking when Mom would tell him we needed to sleep. If I'd gone to sleep before he or Mom got home, I would often hear them fighting in the living room late into the night, their shadows shifting on the wooden floor illuminated by the stray light under the doorway.

Jerry left to study in London and it became slightly easier to deal with him at that distance, when I knew that he couldn't touch me or harm me. But though he was no longer a constant, I would be pinged with his existence each time I received an email or IM from him, and his shadow would loom over me even from afar. If I overheard a laugh that even slightly resembled Jerry's, I would instantly be transported back to our pitch-black bedroom. I would suddenly catch a whiff of that scent, feel the scritch-scritch-scratch of his nails, hear the lingering echoes of his booming laughter.

//

Being trapped at home, my only access to the outside world was my desktop computer. My mother was not pleased by my growing internet addiction, but she allowed it on the basis of helping me get ahead in school. I would spend hours glued to my desk, a row of messenger notifications blinking, multiple windows open to online forums and journal communities back when browser tabs were not yet a thing. In the digital world I wasn't Melissa. I was Neri Son.

As Melissa, I had to be prim and proper, disciplined, an academic role model. As Neri, I could be as wild, silly, and hyper as I wanted. In real life, I wasn't physically active, cute, or attractive, nor could I really stand up to my bullies. Neri, though, could join fighting tournaments and wield a cannon that could launch heavy hardback books into her enemies' faces. I couldn't really go anywhere outside my own house. Neri got to explore all sorts of places and meet new people from around the world. Most importantly, I was taught to "learn to love and accept" my family, whereas Neri got to choose her family. On the internet, anybody could become your brother, your sister, your aunt, your uncle — just a quick revision in your bio or a row with icons stating your online family tree, and you were good to go. Most of the time, it was done jokingly and for fun, but little did I know how offhandedly calling someone my sibling would lead to one of the most significant relationships in my life.

In the early days of the internet, there was no such thing as social media. We had dial-up instead of DSL or cable. The only messenger programs available were AOL, Yahoo! Messenger, and MSN Messenger. Google wasn't yet the king of content; instead, I used Excite.com to lead me to The Anime

Turnpike and its cute pink-haired mascot. It was sort of like the yellow pages, a fan-made directory that collected websites on the subculture of Japanese animation, comics, and video games. (To the yellow pages' credit, you never had to wait twenty minutes for a single page to load.) It was on one of these fan shrines, dedicated to the character Son Goten from *Dragonball Z*, that I first learned about EZBoard and web forums, which reigned supreme in terms of community interaction. It was there that I first met Yukio Himura, a brown-haired, brown-eyed boy with a leather jacket, black shirt, and a sword holstered around his shoulder. (At least that was how he was drawn.) I only have a vague recollection of our very first conversation, but I'm pretty sure it involved my own character wrapping his in toilet paper to mummify him before shoving him into a closet. It was a memorable way to introduce myself, to say the least.

Eventually, I learned that his real name was Eren Nguyen, a fourteen-year-old Vietnamese boy who lived in Madera, California. He had a best friend who was kind of a dick and a father who was really hard on him. Though our first interaction may have been awkward, we soon bonded over our common love for Son Goten and *Dragonball Z*. We both loved anime, the *Final Fantasy* series, drawing, and writing. We played a game of guessing if the other person was drinking water and then making them laugh so they'd snort it out their nose. (We were still two kids on the internet.) Whenever one of us would be in the middle of typing a thought, the other would be able to finish it, as if we could read each other's minds across the Pacific Ocean. Whenever one of us was sad, we somehow could sense it even if neither of us were anywhere close to our computers.

This prompted us to joke that we were psychic siblings, but we both knew that we had a connection beyond those that traveled through cables and wires.

> Neri: That makes you my kuya. Tagalog for 'older brother.'
> Yukio: Well, you're my imouto, then. 'Little sister' in Japanese.
> Neri: Should I call you 'niichan instead?
> Yukio: 'niichan, huh? :) I like the sound of that.

None of us were fluent Japanese speakers, but in our fandom, everyone tended to replace the "o" in "oniichan" with an apostrophe. It may not be proper usage, but we keep it to this day as part of the endearment. We would chat from dusk till dawn, even with our completely different time zones. I'd be a walking zombie when I'd have to go to class the next morning, but I didn't care. All I looked forward to was running home, hopping into my computer chair, and logging into AIM. I soon associated the beeping notifications, the white glow of the screen, and the clackety-clackety-clackety of my keyboard with Eren, with safety. Online, I could be anybody I wanted — even somebody else's younger sister. And suddenly, being stuck at home was no longer torture. I had found a home within my so-called home.

//

How is the kid? Jerry asks as he slides into the backseat. I frown. *I am right here, you know.* I am not "sister." I am not "sibling." I am not Melissa, or Missy, or Mel, or *his*, not even *your,* not even *her.* As we walk up the stairs to our house, he addresses Mom once more: *What's up with the kid?*

I tell him *I have a name.* He laughs and asks, *Is that so?*

//

My mother never told me about the father I never met. As far as I knew, he never existed. Even more curious was that whenever someone rang the doorbell, she'd hide me away in our room. She taught me never to answer the door or the phone if I was home alone. Though I was young, I put two and two together and figured something was going on. But whenever I tried to ask her about him, she'd always dodge the question. When I was older, even getting her drunk with wine wouldn't get a peep out of her.

Jerry also avoided talking about him. *Ask your mother,* he'd say, and I'd raise my brow at the odd use of "your" instead of "our." Once at a bar, both he and Mom got drunk, and Jerry jokingly told her to tell the kid "the story." This prompted my mother to burst into tears, saying that I wasn't ready for "the story" yet. I had a feeling I knew what it was about, but since both of them had a history of yelling at me when drunk, I chose not to pry further.

Despite my best efforts, none of my relatives — not even my mother's best friend — would say a word to me about my father. And because nobody in my real life would tell me the truth I longed for, I opened up about "the story" (that is, the only one I knew: mine) to my friends online. I wanted to make sense of it, to understand why they acted the way they did. I wrote probably a hundred journal entries, locked away on LiveJournal, buried in AIM logs, based on the few nuggets of (supposed) truth I had: that my IRL best friend at the time overheard my *yaya* telling someone that my father already had another family, that he already had other kids, that he was a doctor just like my mother was. This *yaya* openly told a complete stranger, but not me, the child who deserved to know. Nobody told me anything. I thought maybe it was because I didn't matter, and I soon came to believe that I was a mistake. That I was just a glitch in the system. That I was never meant to be here at all.

//

Mel: Eren, I think I have depression.
Eren: I believe you. I think I might have it, too.
Mel: Oh … I don't know what to do.
Eren: Maybe you can look for a therapist?
Mel: Okay … I'll try.

//

What do you want to do, then, my mother roars from the bedroom door as I lie on the bed, hiding under the blankets. *Are you saying you're crazy? What do you want me to do, bring you to a quack to get you checked?*

I cry out *no, no, no, never mind, forget I asked,* shielding my face as she continues to scream at me: *why can't you trust me, have I not been a good mother, you're giving me so much trouble, you know.* Eventually she storms off, slamming the door, and only then do I allow myself to break down into tears on my pillow. I decide then and there it was a stupid idea to try and look for a therapist — how *dare* I ask for help when all of my suffering was obviously my own fault. As soon as I collect myself, I drag my fifteen-year-old self off the bed and toward my computer, and, still sniffling, begin typing:

> Mood: crushed
> I don't even know why I'm still here.

//

One day, when I was about twenty or twenty-one, my then-boyfriend came over to the house. *Yaya* was being verbally abusive to me, and my boyfriend confronted her in an attempt to stand up for me. We had a huge shouting match, I screamed at her to leave, and then fired her, which pissed Jerry off. He offered me an exchange: let *yaya* back in the house, and he would give me information about my father. Jerry taunted me, saying I was possibly an *anak sa labas*, a child out of wedlock. That we never had the same father at all. That we were step-siblings. That I had nothing to do with my mother and my purported father divorcing. But if I wanted to know the truth, my mom and *yaya*'s aversion to house visitors had something to do with me and with my dad. All I had to do was do what he wanted, even though he knew — he *knew* — it would destroy my mental and emotional health. Letting an emotionally abusive employee back into our house was never going to be good for me. But when it came to choosing between firing *yaya* or blaming me, the person who was actually flesh and blood family, Jerry chose the latter. I was the spoiled brat. I was the ungrateful one. I should just shut up and let *yaya* back into the house. It didn't help that my mother sided with *yaya*, too, telling me I was giving her a ton of trouble by firing someone she needed.

//

I am twenty-three and in the middle of the Palawan airport lobby with my mother, Jerry, *yaya*, and some other relatives. We are on the last day of our vacation (one that I reluctantly agreed to join), waiting to be called for our flight back home to Manila.

Jerry turns his head toward me and, gnashing his teeth, tells me to shut the fuck up.

He says it three times, crisp and loud and stinging. I stare at him in disbelief. My eyes scan the room: my relatives say nothing as Jerry continues to curse me. I fight back tears and pull my luggage to board the plane. My mother catches up and scolds me for starting a fight. I lose what little composure I have left and scream at her to leave me alone. This takes her aback, and she stays silent for the rest of the trip. I cry on the entire flight back, contemplating how to erase myself as soon as we arrive home.

//

It seemed like any other day. I lay in bed, once again alone in our shared bedroom, staring at the ceiling as the wall clock above our vanity mirror ticked, ticked, ticked.

And then I started to cry. Heaved. It was a long sob, sustained by a deep, encompassing sadness, and for a moment I succumbed to the thought that I didn't deserve to be here — that I was never meant to exist in the first place. That I should be less of a burden to everybody. That I should make myself disappear. I felt like I was sinking into the mattress, enveloped by a dark mass I couldn't muster the energy to resist. I felt like I was about to lose myself, lose my senses, disappear for good. And I knew that there was nobody at home to help me. Not knowing what else to do, my first instinct was to reach for my iPhone 3Gs and scroll through my contact list to look for Eren.

If my phone hadn't been within reach . . . if Eren hadn't been online . . . I wouldn't be here typing this essay today.

//

Eren believed I should try going to a therapist again. At the time, I couldn't afford it. I couldn't tell my mother, fearing another screaming match. I thought of starting a fundraiser, but felt that I didn't deserve to be helped. I hadn't even opened up about my depression yet, either; it was something I hesitated to share on Facebook, which was mostly populated by people I actually knew IRL. I never talked about my mental health there, feeling only that Dreamwidth and LiveJournal were fit for those kinds of deeply personal thoughts. But Eren convinced me to give it a try, reassured me that I was worth helping, told me he would always be there to support me even if we were continents apart. Because no matter what happened, regardless of anything Jerry ever said to me, Eren loved me and wanted me to stay.

So, that night, shaking and my palms ice-cold, I launched the fundraiser. And within a few minutes, donations started to pour in. People shared my status, left me supportive comments, met up with me to hand me money. Even complete strangers started donating to the fundraiser. In that moment, overwhelmed by the help of everybody on the internet — both people I had never met, and people I knew well IRL — I started to cry, this time not out of sorrow but out of relief, of joy, of gratitude. That night I had made myself seen, made myself the most visible I'd been, laid bare all my psychological scars to the public — scars I'd only shown friends in the privacy of access-locked entries of LiveJournal or Dreamwidth. But what surprised me the most was that people began to reach out to me through private messages to ask for *my* help, because they thought that they, too, might have been silently suffering from depression. By being open about my own mental health struggles, I had given them the courage to try to seek help for their conditions, too. To this day, friends still message me saying I am the only person they know who has been open about declaring their depression, the only person they felt they could turn to for help. All because my brother Eren sent an instant message urging me to hang on, telling me not to give up, insisting that I deserved to be here. All because he believed in me. All because I was his *imouto*.

//

Going to therapy at twenty-three changed my life. It was as if the dark shadow had been lifted and the burden of justifying my existence had been taken off my shoulders. Through therapy I was able to process the thoughts I'd been struggling with in private LJ entries, dumping them in a messy metaphorical heap all over my therapist's desk. We sorted through the trauma I'd gone through, and I was encouraged to put up more boundaries, including against my family. This advice echoed much of what my friends online had told me, that I had to extract myself from that toxic situation so that I could shake off all the lies and negativity that had been thrown at me growing up.

I cut ties with Jerry for good. My mother was upset, unable to understand why I'd disown my supposed blood brother. Maybe I hadn't tried hard enough, we were all adults here,

hadn't I already moved on by now, wouldn't I do it for *her*?
With my newfound confidence, I made it clear that I *had* tried
it numerous times, I *had* done it for her, I *had* put up with it *for
over twenty years*. I needed space from him in order to slowly
regain my mental health. I preferred to invest in a relationship
with somebody I had never touched, seen, or been in the same
room with than with someone who breathed the same air as me,
yet treated me like I wasn't another human worthy of respect
and dignity.

I was incredibly privileged to have access to the web
during such trying times. Thanks to the early internet's rel-
ative obscurity, it functioned as a safe space, a reprieve from
the daily woes of everyday life. Online fandom communities
were places where you could do or be anything; they gave
you permission to explore identities, discover others who had
the same experiences, and even to find — and choose — your
own families. Heck, the internet allowed a Vietnamese boy
in California to reach a Filipina in the Philippines just in
the nick of time.

I met people who wouldn't judge me for the suffering I went
through, who validated my concerns, who listened to me and
pulled me through whenever I was engulfed by the darkness.
Close-knit internet communities introduced me to people from
other walks of life, made me aware of struggles different from
mine, and taught me how to have empathy for others. But more
than anything, I believed — I still believe — in the internet's
capability to bring you closer to the people you need, the people
that you would never have known existed, to allow you to form
important connections that would have otherwise been physically impossible. Internet communities are a lifeline for when

the offline world fails you — they have the capacity to save you. It wouldn't be an exaggeration to say that the internet saved *me*.

//

Mel: Eren? Are you free?

Eren: Yeah. Why?

Nervously, I type:

Mel: Do you wanna try a video call?

Eren: :) Of course. I'd love to.

The Skype ringtone plays. I press Accept.

Hi, Mel! Can you see me?

I immediately cover my face and squeak.

Are you okay? If you're uncomfortable . . .

I gulp.

Just . . . give me a moment.

I peek from between my fingers. I see Eren's short black hair, slanted eyes, skin with a colour close to mine.

Eren waves.

Hello, imouto! *I love you.*

I slowly take my hands away and smile.

Hello, kuya. *I love you, too.*

THE RESTAURANT AT THE END OF THE INTERNET

Andy Connor

In July of 2004, a woolly-jumpered New Zealander named Chanel Cole was emptying her water bottle into Sydney Harbour. When the television host asked why she should be the next Australian Idol, she looked directly into the camera and replied, "Because I think there is a severe lack of articulate, brunette, size 12, flat-chested women on television."

Something about her made me sit up straighter on the couch. At the time, I was a mutedly sad fifteen-year-old living in a country Victoria town, good at debate but bad at conversation, uncomfortable being a boy but with no words for that yet. I would have told you that I watched Australian Idol with a certain amount of ironic distance — "as trash" — but that posture didn't last. Chanel began her audition by deliberately sounding like one of the pitchy disasters they let on just to laugh at them ("I've just gotta find my note ... "), but then suavely transitioned into a flawless Ella Fitzgerald. By the time she sung Portishead in the semifinals, I was toast. I'd never seen anyone as clever and compelling as her on TV, and I drank up every moment she was on screen.

Because my family liked Australian Idol, we were allowed to call in and vote for our favourite — but only once per week. This was grossly inadequate, in my view, and I began sneaking in extra votes for Chanel whenever I could. I shared a room with my brother, and so after our usual meandering pre-sleep chats, I'd lie in bed with my eyes stretched open, which was just uncomfortable enough to keep me awake until I could hear my brother's snores. I came to know which floorboards in our old house were snitches and padded past my parents' room quietly enough that I never once woke them. I had a notion that if I voted *too* much I'd be caught, so I kept myself carefully restrained. Five votes here, seven votes there; never more than ten at a time. I just wanted her to stay on the show so badly. I wanted her to keep showing me how you could be weird and still survive with your humour and happiness intact.

The official Yahoo! Australian Idol forums were a place of stark Hobbesian chaos. There were no moderators, zero mechanisms for blocking or banning people, and a pervasive ethos of turf war. All the different Idol contestants had their own subforums, but rather than being a home base for fans, the list of threads tended to read like hate-filled graffiti: fans of *other* contestants doing drive-by shit-talking and drowning out any positive takes. The Chanel Cole subforum was no different: a scoured battleground, plagued by raiding parties from the Anthony Callea and RickiLee Coulter subforums (where, I can only assume, the sun never shone and the living envied the dead). But in amongst the pandemonium, I saw an interesting form of resistance.

Led by an enigmatic and fascinating poster named sunshine (who we all called Sunny) there was a small group of people on the Chanel board who, whenever somebody made an all-caps post about how Chanel was a sucky loser who sucked, would reply, "Aw, thanks! We love you too!" Often, the troll would reply almost touchingly earnestly, trying to correct the misunderstanding — "No, um, I actually *hate* you, where did you get confused?" — and the Chanel fans would blithely keep on replying as if the troll had just expressed something sweet and loving. It was strangely effective, and (posting under the name The_Rumpled_Academic), I joined in the game. It felt satisfying to stymie them, and Chanel kept not getting eliminated, so I began to sense a superstitious connection between the two. Somehow, I intuited that us being there was helping her survive on the show. We were her vanguard, weeding out the trolls with tactical affection, depolluting the soil so she could take root.

One night, a Chanelite named revolution_rose came up with an even better tactic. She made a post announcing that, since she was a financially comfortable baby boomer with nothing on her hands but time and a nice glass of Sauvignon Blanc, she would call in and vote for Chanel *every single time* she saw a troll post. It was the kind of gambit that would make the narrator of a military documentary breathless; it completely scrambled them. Every time a trollish partisan posted something awful, revolution_rose would thank them for giving her an excuse to vote for Chanel again. They'd try to get back the upper hand (by declaring that they didn't believe her, or mocking her for wasting her money, or posting disguised links to goatse), and she'd just cheerily inform them that, sure enough, she'd just voted again. It wasn't long before all the trolls had fled, fearing this profligate madwoman and her undefeatable jiu-jitsu.

This was when the real fun began. To keep revolution_rose voting, the rest of us spent the night creating dummy accounts, posting the silliest and most obvious trolls we could think of, and melodramatically lamenting all the votes we were causing her to cast. As the night went on, our trolling got increasingly hammy and esoteric, culminating in someone posting a version of Martin Luther's Ninety-Five Theses modified to froth with Protestant rage at Chanel, that demon of demons. Entirely in on the joke, revolution_rose kept letting us know that, yep, she'd voted again — and again, and again, all night — until, she told us the next morning, she finally dozed off in her armchair, her smile as full as her phone bill.

It used to be conventional wisdom that it was the anonymity of the internet that made people act like trolls. Then Facebook taught us that people are startlingly willing to be vicious little shits with their real name and face attached, so that explanation lost its neatness. Now that advertisers track us all over the internet, it's a little easier to see what we were taking for granted in 2005. It's easier to see the social and introspective *upsides* of anonymity. It's easier to see the way that not being pinned to your 'real life' can allow you to be more honest about what that life is lacking, and more imaginative in figuring out how to fill it.

With the subforum almost fully weeded of trolls, the Chanelites — like an off-duty regiment having a coffee klatsch between missions — finally got the chance to talk. Conversations about Chanel morphed into conversations about art; conversations about art to conversations about childhood; conversations about childhood to conversations about Trotsky's concept of permanent revolution. On that board were the first openly gay people I ever met, as well as the first closeted trans people. There was an Argentinian-Israeli maths teacher, a Nietzschean Buddhist antifa goth, and a hysterically funny single mum from Perth. We talked about Bananarama and Baudrillard, about bullies and bulimia, and I began to wonder if this was what people meant when they talked about community.

The longest thread on the Chanel subforum was a creation of mine: "Rumpy's Restaurant." It grew out of something watt_tyler used to do in the general chat thread, where he'd come in after a long day and write *pours glass of cognac* before getting into it. Pretty soon we were all swept up in the gentle roleplay of the restaurant. People would come in and ask for whatever food or drink they wanted, and and I — as the 'owner' of the restaurant — would serve it up for them. It was a general chat thread, but also something more distinct. People talked about the Restaurant like it was a place, like it was their *favourite* place. It was a warm wooden lamplit space that always welcomed you, where your friends were always either there or coming back soon.

It's 2004, and watt_tyler is telling me about Spinoza for the first time, a decade before I'd go on to do a master's in philosophy.

It's 2010, and watt — Yair — has finally convinced me to come with him to a soccer game. He wants me to understand the comradeship of the lunatics who chant in the north terrace all game long. I tell him I do understand, but only because "They're basically Chanelites, right?"

It's 2015, and Yair's talking me though his cancer diagnosis. The nurses and doctors are apologetic that the only reading material they can give him about breast cancer is pink and flowery and clearly written for women. He laughs and says it's the least of his problems.

The Yahoo! message boards closed down after the season ended, but the Chanelites didn't. Sunny and JB set up a new forum, chanelcole.cc (now an official fan club, with an ACN and a constitution), and most of us made the migration. We held meetups, crowdfunded Chanel's first CD — long before 'crowd-funding' was a term any of us had in our vocabulary — and got even more involved in each other's lives. There was a new Rumpy's Restaurant, and then another one, and then another, each running hundreds of pages long.

One regular at Rumpy's Restaurant, a motherly Christian lady named PurpleGracieGirl, thought my vocabulary was suspiciously large for a fifteen-year-old and decided to do a little digging. She found a middle-aged doctor in rural Victoria with my name and thought "Aha! This must be Rumpy, pretending to be fifteen online for the attention." She sent him a very stern email concluding with a righteous ultimatum: "If you don't tell everyone the truth, I will." The poor doctor sent her back an utterly bewildered response, and Purps was mortified.

She only told me about any of this years later, after we'd finally met in person and the very last of her suspicions had been put to rest. I love this story. It's exactly the kind of thing that was facilitated by this era of the internet: a million opportunities to be suspicious, but also the occasional deep-crimson pleasure of having 'too good to be' turn out to be true.

It's 2006, and my brother is moving to Sydney to be with his girlfriend, rocketfox, who he met on chanelcole.cc. We listen to the Flaming Lips' *Zaireeka* on three stereos and a PlayStation, and everything seems perfect.

It's 2007, and our band is playing our first-ever show in a crowded backyard, with Alicey from the forum on cello.

It's 2019, and Sunny and Lakey are saving money for their wedding. "We already consider ourselves married, but we want to do it right," Sunny tells me. Plus, after fourteen years and a gender transition, "I look awesome in a tux."

One night that stands out in my memory: Yair and I tag-teaming an explanation of the Russian Revolution for a curious fourteen-year-old who asked us what we were talking about. We were succinct in our answers early on, but then she kept asking more questions, so then we let loose. We went all the way from Bloody Sunday through the Kornilov Affair and the October Revolution, concluding well after midnight with Trotsky's assassination. She kept saying how fascinating and sad it all was, and how she couldn't believe she'd never heard any of this stuff before. Years later, she'd go on to do a BA in history, and Yair and I quietly high-fived in our PMs.

Weekly trivia nights in the chatroom. Jokey forum games stretching hundreds of pages. These miraculous mixtape swaps, where you'd get assigned a person to mail a mixtape or mix-CD to, and someone else would be assigned to send one to you, and it would all end up in this big adoring circle. I vividly remember cutting open the padded envelope and removing the CD that Timoth had burned for me, feeling like an acolyte entrusted with the ashes of a saint. It was packed to the brim with 700 megabytes of Neu, Diamanda Galás, Godspeed You! Black Emperor, Autechre, Mr Bungle — everything a warped and concentrated version of itself, a spell for summoning new shapes I could evolve into.

As far as I've been able to research, there are seven couples who met on chanelcole.cc who are still together in 2019. They're mostly queer women — as most of the forum was — and for a couple of them, it was their coming-out relationship. I never dated anyone from the forum, but there was this curious running joke between me and fevveryfevs (a girl my age from Melbourne) where we play-acted like we were married. People sometimes thought that it portended something, but it never seemed to me in any danger of porting to reality. Our playmarriage was companionate and dodderingly sexless, like the old couple in *When the Wind Blows*. She called me "hubbie," and I called her "honeybunch." She photoshopped me saccharine Valentines, and I fetched wood for the fire. I felt like trying to make it real would ruin it, which in retrospect is how I felt about a lot of things.

Everyone on the forums seemed so excited at the prospect of meetups, but I was apprehensive. I was so much more comfortable being the words that I typed; I felt sure that they were more likeable and interesting than I was capable of being IRL. The internet has always been "real life" — of course — but it used to more easily facilitate the feeling of *multiple* lives, each as real as the other. On cc.cc, I was more myself than I could ever afford to be at my school: more vulnerable, kinder, more curious about what's going on inside other people. It wasn't a fantasy or a false life or a distraction; it was me practicing myself into existence.

It's 2005, and I'm posting on the forum about my first kiss.

It's 2015, and I'm crying into Timoth's shoulder at the funeral of a friend. Later, outside the wake, I read him an Adrienne Rich poem off my phone ("within us and against us, against us and within us"), and he hugs me hard.

It's 2019, and I'm getting back in touch with people to write this piece. There's about a dozen I still have on Facebook. I ask for recollections and receive long, scattered messages back, everyone recalling different things. There were things I never even knew about, like the forum providing relationship references for immigration papers, and the mods locating a homeless shelter for a young forum member who'd been kicked out of home. I ask for artefacts and get sent old photos, LiveJournals links, and even some of the custom Chanel-themed forum smileys we used to use. I'm absolutely smitten with the smileys. It may just be nostalgia, but I can't help but feel that they have unusually kind eyes.

The culmination of the forum was Colestock 2005: this big, weekend-long meetup held in Chanel's hometown of Bega. My parents, astonishingly, let me and my brother go by ourselves, and even more astonishingly, nothing bad happened. We met a bunch of sweet, awkward people, thrilled at hearing our forum in-jokes said out loud, and ate an ungodly amount of cheese. We hung out with Chanel — who was just a person, who was lovely, who recognised intuitively

that this community had become about more than her — and
sang karaoke deep into the night. On the final night, we had
a huge meal at a restaurant with all of us, and someone had
printed out custom menus to replace the restaurant's usual
ones. They said "Rumpy's Restaurant," and my heart went
supernova when I saw them.

There's something so *off* about the fact that the real Rumpy's
Restaurants — the megathreads, first on Yahoo! and then cha-
nelcole.cc — have vanished, and yet this menu is still around,
tucked in a box under my bed. At the time, it felt so clear to us
where the reality lay. The Restaurants were these authentic,
scuffed, lived-in places. Flirtations turned into relationships
there. Conversations became conversions. "Jokes" became
genders. The menu didn't feel like it was making the restaurant "real"; it was simply a sweet, in-jokey reference to a site of
community alchemy that we all already knew to be real. But
now, the real Restaurants are gone. They were never archived
by the Wayback Machine — never saved anywhere, as far as
I can tell — and the only hard evidence they ever even existed
is this one piece of stock paper, signed for me by Chanel, from
the one night when the Restaurant turned corporeal.

There is one other physical remnant of chanelcole.cc that
I know of. When the admins organised Colestock, they kept
accepting donations even after all the expenses had been covered. After it was all finished, they decided to donate everything
that was left over to the Bega Hospital. Apparently, it was just
enough to buy a newborn incubation cradle   which is still
there, in that regional hospital in New South Wales, with a
small plaque on it that reads, "DONATED BY THE CHANEL
COLE FAN CLUB."

CONTRIBUTORS

Erica Buist is a journalist, lecturer, and author. Formerly a staffer at the Guardian, her writing has also been published in The Sunday Times, the BBC, Medium, the Mirror, and various literary magazines. She has been a writer-in-residence at the Wellstone Center in the Redwoods, Vermont Studio Center, Faber, Arte Studio Ginestrelle, and Virginia Center for the Creative Arts. Erica regularly appears on BBC Radio, and is currently writing a nonfiction book called *This Party's Dead*, to be published in 2021 by Unbound. She speaks five languages, mostly to her dog.

Mimi Mondal is a science fiction and fantasy writer and editor from India, who primarily lives online. Her co-edited anthology *Luminescent Threads: Connections to Octavia E. Butler* won a Locus Award and was nominated for a Hugo Award in 2018. She currently writes a futurism/politics/culture column called "Extraordinary Alien" on Hindustan Times and a history/myth/worldbuilding column called "Other Indias" on her Patreon.

Damien Patrick Williams has a master's degree in philosophy and comparative religious studies, with a focus on occult systems, and a master's degree in science and technology studies, in which he is also pursuing a doctorate. He explores how philosophy, technology, religious traditions, public policy, and society all intersect, and considers our values, intentions, and behaviours regarding genetic manipulation, biomechanical alterations, and algorithmic, internet-connected systems.

Sisonke Msimang is a South African who writes about culture, power, sex, and money. She is the author of two books — *Always Another Country: A Memoir of Exile and Home* (2017), and *The Resurrection of Winnie Mandela* (2018).

Ryan North wrote Dinosaur Comics, the Eisner award-winning *Adventure Time* comics, the #1 bestselling anthology series *Machine of Death,* and the New York Times-bestselling and Eisner-award winning *Unbeatable Squirrel Girl* series for Marvel. He's turned Shakespeare into NYT-bestselling choose-your-own-path books that allows YOU to play through and make the decisions for Shakespeare's heroes, which is absolutely a great idea and won't cause them to get into trouble three choices in. His latest book, *How to Invent Everything*, is a complete cheat sheet for civilisation. He once messed up walking his dog so badly it made the news.

Anaïs Escobar Mathers is an editor and writer living in Toronto. Her work has also appeared in This Recording and One Week// One Band over the years. She is best known for her blog, You've Escaped, which has transitioned into a Tinyletter of the same name. She is currently working on a selection of new essays about chronic illness and social media.

James Mitchell is a writer and performer of science fiction, magical realism, and true stories. He graduated from the Birkbeck Creative Writing MA in 2015, and since then has spent his time trying to smuggle odd tales into places like Vice, GQ, and the vacant fourth plinth of Trafalgar Square. In 2019 he won the inaugural Brick Lane Bookshop Short Story Prize. He lives in London. Read his work at jamesmitchell.persona.co. He still reads "A Wish For Jackie," looking for clues to the man who wrote it — ask him @jamescmitchell, and he'll share it with you.

Mohale Mashigo is the author of the bestselling, award-winning novel *The Yearning* (2016) and a collection of speculative fiction stories *Intruders* (2018). Mohale was born and raised in Soweto; she is a mutli-disciplinary storyteller who loves exploring the unknown. She currently resides in what she describes as a sleepy suburb of Cape Town "where people either retire or start families." Mashigo holds a BA (Journalism & Lingistuics) degree from Rhodes University. She is also author of a YA novel adaptation of the film *Beyond the River* and she writes for the comic book series *Kwezi* (South Africa's first superhero).

Kaite Welsh is an author, critic, and journalist living in Scotland. Her series of Victorian feminist mysteries starring medical student, fallen woman, and amateur sleuth Sarah Gilchrist has been praised by the New York Times and she is a former Daily Telegraph columnist focusing on LGBT issues. Her journalism has appeared in the Guardian, CNN, and the New Statesman, among others, and she is Books Editor at DIVA Magazine. She also makes frequent appearances on BBC TV and radio discussing feminist and cultural issues. Kaite is represented by Laura Macdougall at United Artists.

Lola Keeley is a writer and coder. After moving to London to pursue her love of theatre, she later wound up living every five-year-old's dream of being a train driver on the London Underground. She has since emerged, blinking into the sunlight, to find herself writing books. She now lives in Edinburgh, Scotland, with her wife and four cats.

Leah Reich is a writer and researcher. She lives in New York City with her cat, Lumpy.

Kyle Cassidy is a writer and visual artist from West Philadelphia who spends his time documenting subcultures. He's the author of *Armed America: Portraits of Gun Owners in Their Homes, This is What a Librarian Looks Like* and *War Paint: Tattoo Culture and the Armed Forces*. He's also done extensive series on oil workers, scientists, F&SF fans, novelists and protesters. He started blogging on January 1, 2000 with his Photo-A-Week series and hasn't stopped. In 2010 he was elected User Representative to the board of the social media site LiveJournal. Currently he's writing a book about the invention of the payphone.

Randell Zuleka Dauda is from Liberia. She relocated to the US during the Liberian Crisis. She is a full-time PhD student in Planning, Governance and Globalization at Virginia Tech and a passionate storyteller online. Randell firmly believes in changing Africa's narrative by giving Africans the opportunity to tell their own stories. In her spare time, she curates stories about various parts of Liberia to counter the narrative of Africa as a jungle. She is a headwrap enthusiast and uses African print to bring awareness to her work and culture. If you are on Instagram, check out @Zuleka_.

Odds are nonzero that somehow, you know someone who knows Jon Sung. When not dodging errant LiDAR beams and frothing venture capitalists in the heart of Silicon Valley, Jon splits his time between raising his kid, wrangling words for clients, and recording a podcast with his friends that searches a dozen+ years' worth of ideas for gold, absurdity, and/or occasional horror. Find and follow Jon and his work at flavor.country.

Molly Crabapple is a New York-based artist and writer. She is the author of *Drawing Blood* and *Brothers of the Gun* (with Marwan Hisham), which was longlisted for a National Book Award. Her reportage has been published in the New York Times, New York Review of Books, Vanity Fair, the Guardian, Rolling Stone, and elsewhere. She has been the recipient of a Yale Poynter Fellowship, a Front Page Award, and shortlisted for a Frontline Print Journalism Award. Her art is in the permanent collections of the Museum of Modern Art, the Library of Congress, and the New York Historical Society.

Melissa Gira Grant is a senior staff reporter covering criminal justice at The Appeal and the author of *Playing the Whore: The Work of Sex Work* (Verso). She has been a contributing writer at the Village Voice and Pacific Standard, and her work has also appeared in the Guardian, the New York Times, Buzz-Feed News, the New York Review of Books, and the Nation, among others. Her essays are collected in *Best Sex Writing,* *The Feminist Utopia Project,* and *Where Freedom Starts: Sex Power Violence #MeToo.* She lives in New York.

Catherine Tan is a writer and poet exploring the intersections of mental health, identity, and diversity through folklore and mythology. In her free time, she can be found knee-deep in fandom and gaming culture. She is currently @mx.nepenthe on Instagram, where she is relearning how to do social media.

Jadzia Axelrod is the author and illustrator behind *Franken-stein's Support Group For Misunderstood Monsters,* a comic about monsters and feelings, for Quirk Books. She is the writer and producer of the award-winning podcast, "The Voice Of Free Planet X," where she interviews stranded time-travelers, low-rent superheroes, unrepentant monsters, and other such creatures of sci-fi and fantasy. She is not domestic, she is a luxury, and in that sense, necessary.

Jessica Val Ang is a 5'0 pocket rocket. Translator by day, crea-tive by night. Passionate about photography and travel. Believes in sustainable lifestyles and that food is medicine. Ex-sci-fi/fantasy geek. Thinks spiders are adorable. She can be found on Instagram @jessicaval.

Thomas Pluck is the author of the Anthony-finalist crime novel *Bad Boy Boogie,* the adventure novel *Blade of Dishonor,* and dozens of stories and essays that have appeared every-where from to LitHub to The Utne Reader. He has slung hash, worked on the docks, and trained in mixed martial arts in Japan and the United States. Joyce Carol Oates calls him "a lovely kitty man."

Kaitlin Tremblay is a writer and video game developer. She was the lead writer on the death-positive video game *A Mortician's Tale* (Laundry Bear, 2017) and was a lead narrative designer on *Watch Dogs Legion* (Ubisoft Toronto). She is the author of the book on subversive storytelling in video games *Ain't No Place For A Hero: Borderlands* (ECW Press, 2017), and she was the co-editor on *Those Who Make Us: Canadian Creature, Myth, and Monster Stories* (Exile Editions, 2016). Kaitlin is a co-director of the feminist non-profit Dames Making Games and is currently a writer at Capybara Games.

Charles Pulliam-Moore is a New York-based writer living a double life as a news reporter and culture critic for io9 who focuses on comic books, movies, and television shows. His work covering a broad variety of topics — including race, technology, queerness, and representation in pop culture — has been fea-tured on NPR, PBS Newshour, and in Slate magazine.

Mel G. Cabral is a bi non-binary Filipina creative. By day, they are a content writer, direct response copywriter, and digital marketing consultant. By night, they are a creative writer, editor, illustrator, graphic designer, and art merchant. They are an advocate for LGBTQ+ rights, mental health support, fair pay for creatives, and productive self-care. In their downtime, they like to craft, cook, play games, cry over fictional characters, and dream up new projects with their partner and friends. They are also a member of the Filipino artist circle Merllamas and in charge of Operations at StickerVault. Find out more at melgcabral.com.

Andy Connor is a nonbinary writer living in Melbourne, Australia. A jack of entirely too many trades, Andy's done stand-up, written essays and comics and poetry, played drums in a moderately successful indie band, authored an advice column in the character of a cartoon moose, and written a philosophy master's thesis about love and abuse. They've been published in the Guardian, The Lifted Brow, Overland, The Suburban Review, Scum Mag, Going Down Swinging, and others. For a day job, Andy works as a court transcriptionist.

ACKNOWLEDGEMENTS

This book was proudly funded through Kickstarter, a platform that allows people to pledge their support to various types of creative projects from around the world. Kickstarter is useful for independent artists of all kinds to help them continue to make weird and wonderful work that otherwise wouldn't exist. Thank you to everyone who backed this book. Without your support, generosity, and passion for it, it would never have happened.

It is absolutely beautiful that a book about finding your people on the internet was made possible by a bunch of people who found it on the internet.

We made this this book because we wanted to honour the internet that created us; take a long look at it and try to learn something new from our own histories; make an offering to the internet pioneers and participants and just say, thank you. We are who we are because of you. Thank you for convincing us not to log off. :)

<3
Katie West
Founder, Fiction & Feeling

First published with Fiction & Feeling
and now published with Weiser Books

BECOMING DANGEROUS
edited by Katie West and Jasmine Elliott

Edgy and often deeply personal, the essays collected in this anthology come from a wide variety of contributors. Some identify as witches; others as writers, musicians, game developers, or artists. What they have in common is that they've created personal rituals to summon their own power in a world that would prefer them powerless. Here, they share the practices they use to resist self-doubt, grief, and depression in the face of sexism, slut-shaming, racism, patriarcy, and other system of oppression.

Replete with prose that is at turns revealing, relatable, and bitingly funny, this book lays the groundwork for summoning your own salvation on your own terms.
Kristen J. Sollée
author of *Witches, Sluts, Feminists: Conjuring the Sex Positive*

Thoughtful and earnest, considered together these essays weave a spell, taking the acts of women deemed selfish and silly and naming them sacred. Witches are having a moment. And it's about damn time.
Kelly Sue DeConnick
author of *Bitch Planet, Pretty Deadly*

WEISER BOOKS
redwheelweiser.com

SPLIT

true stories about the end of marriage and what happens next

edited by Katie West and Jasmine Elliott

Tell someone you're divorced and they look at you differently. The pity, shame, and sense of failing at something that was only supposed to end in death can be a heavy burden to bear. But it doesn't have to be. This book collects essays written by divorced writers exploring what led them to divorce, how they lived through it, and, perhaps most importantly, who they are now that it's over.

SPLIT is filled with humanity and honesty on a rarely discussed subject. Each writer approaches their story in their own way, while the book still feels cohesive as a whole. By the end, the word I was thinking wasn't split, it was hope.
RoguesPortal.com

There are stories in this book from the conventional to the positively twenty-first century, from the upbeat to the equally down tempo, from recovered souls and people still finding their way. In every case there is a new truth about human relationships waiting to be found by the reader.
C. Oliver Godby

fictionandfeeling.com

For more from Fiction & Feeling

FOLLOW US ON TWITTER
@fictionfeeling

FIND US ON INSTAGRAM
@fictionandfeeling

VISIT OUR WEBSITE AND
SIGN UP TO OUR NEWSLETTER
fictionandfeeling.com

If you enjoyed this book (or any book you read!) leaving a review on Amazon, Goodreads, or with your favourite local bookseller is one of the best ways to make sure other people can enjoy it too. It really helps small independent publishers like us!

&

fiction & feeling